Know Him, Serve Him

Know Him, Serve Him

Discover God's Radical Plan for Your Life

SEAN DUNN

Fleming H. Revell
A Division of Baker Book House Co
Grand Rapids, Michigan 49516

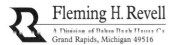

Published by Fleming H. Revell
a division of Baker Book House Company
P.O. Box 6287, Grand Rapids, MI 49516-6287

Printed in the United States of America

Library of Congress Cataloging-in-Publication Data

Dunn, Sean, 1968–
Know Him, Serve Him: discover God's radical plan for your life / Sean Dunn.
p. cm.
Summary: Focuses on helping young people know God on a more intimate level and showing them how to do God's will in their daily lives.
ISBN 0-8007-5819-6 (pbk.)
1. Christian teenagers—Religious life. [1. Christian life. 2. Conduct of life.] I. Title.
BV4531.3 .D865 2002
248.8′3—dc21 2001058599

For current information about all releases from Baker Book House, visit our web site:
http://www.bakerbooks.com

Contents

Part 1

first Things first

You were born to work for God!

You know you have a destiny. You know that God has a calling on your life and you want to fulfill the incredible plans he has laid out for you. Seeing souls saved, needs met, and the gospel preached gets you pumped. You were born to work for God!

Or, maybe you are the type of person who cannot say with confidence that God has big things in store, but you have a heart for God that is huge. Something in you breaks when you think about people who do not know Christ. Your heart is torn when you picture the state of the world. But you're not one of those people who merely points out the need, you want to be there when God answers the need! When God answers prayers and does miracles, you want to be there, not only to watch, but to participate.

If your prayer is that God's kingdom would be built and his Son glorified, this book is for you. By the time you have turned the last page, and read the last words, you will be better equipped to participate in God's plan.

However, it would be a shame to skip the first step in this whole process. We must get first things first, or nothing will come out right.

You are called to make him known, to be effective and to produce lasting fruit, so your first priority must be to know God well. The first several chapters are about getting to know God—his voice, his strategies. If you learn who he is, how to hear him, and what he is most concerned about, you will be effective in making him known.

1

What Do You See?

"Come, follow me," Jesus said, "and I will make you fishers of men."

MATTHEW 4:19

Andrew turned around to see Jesus looking at them. He had never seen anything like this man before. Jesus' gaze captivated his attention and drew him in. The fisherman had been given an invitation to join this man—to walk with him, live with him, eat with him, and learn from him.

One of Andrew's friends saw that he was considering taking this man from Nazareth up on his offer. "You aren't actually thinking about going with this guy, are you?"

The question was asked but not heard. Andrew made up his mind to trust his life to Jesus. He was willing to give up everything he had dreamed for his future because he saw something in Jesus he couldn't ignore.

"Without delay" he left and followed Jesus. "At once" and "immediately" is how the Gospels record Andrew's response to the invitation. There was no hesitation, no indecisiveness. He knew right away that he wanted to be with Jesus; nothing else mattered.

What Did They See in Him?

The men Jesus called from along the beach in Matthew 4 must have seen something special in Jesus, for with few words and very little time to weigh the options, they made a decision that changed the course of their lives. They didn't give up just one day, they laid down their entire future with "no hesitation."

They Saw a Future

Andrew and the others were at the Sea of Galilee working on their nets, having just come in from a day of fishing. They were not fishing for recreation's sake but for their livelihood. Fishing was how they earned their living, fed their families, and had they not met Jesus, it was the course they had chosen for their future.

In a moment all that changed. Jesus walked past and called out to them. His request was simple. "Follow me." Yet the ramifications of their response would change their lives. If they chose to walk with Jesus, they would have to step out of their comfort zones and walk by faith. They would be giving up their occupations and their parts in the family business (Mark 1 records they had hired men). Everything about their daily routine and long-range goals would be revolutionized. But something they saw in Jesus made the decision easy for them.

Although they had very little knowledge of Jesus before this moment, what they saw in him made them willing to trust him with their future. "How can I stay here and fish when I have the chance to go with him?" they may have thought to themselves. "Nothing I have known in the past will compare to what I will know if I follow Jesus."

Something they saw in Jesus made the decision easy for them.

They Saw Love

When the fishermen considered following Jesus, they were willing to give up all of their family relationships. Every source of love and support they had ever known was left behind the day that they set out to follow Jesus.

When they looked at Jesus, they saw something in him that they had never seen before. They saw a love that did not originate on earth, but one that began in heaven. The way that Jesus carried himself, the way he looked at them, and the tone of his voice set these men at ease and drew them in. They wanted to be around that kind of love.

They had known the love of their fathers and mothers. They had been around friends, but there was something unique and inviting in the unspoken yet powerful love that emanated from this man. Even at first glance, they knew there was something in this man that saw the best in them. He did not judge them though he knew all about them. He did not label them by their past failures; because he loved them perfectly, he would help them write better futures.

Something deep inside them wanted to be loved this perfectly, but they had never known unconditional and unlimited love before. When they saw it in Jesus, all of their other relationships were not worth holding on to.

They Saw an Identity

That morning when they woke up, they were fishermen. They had no desire to be anything else, and even if they desired to be something other than men who worked on the open sea, they weren't qualified to do anything other than fish. That all changed the moment they looked at Jesus.

In a split second they were willing to change the way they had been known. Now, instead of being fishermen, they would be known as disciples. Rather than chasing fish, they would be pursuers and servants of Jesus. They would be associated with him, recognized as his own, and defined by their relationship with him.

They embraced this change, because they saw in him one with whom they could trust their reputation. Something convinced them at first look that Jesus would alter their identity and protect their honor.

They Saw a Purpose

Peter, Andrew, James, and John, the men who followed Jesus that day, had always lived to catch fish. This allowed them to make money, which enabled them to feed themselves and their families. In turn, they were able to stay alive to fish some more. This cycle was all they had ever known and although it became mundane and routine, they never questioned it until the day Jesus walked into their lives.

The moment he called to them, they were willing to change their direction. The Lord had a purpose for them and it was more than an endless cycle of fishing to survive. He wanted them to impact their culture and the world.

When Jesus made eye contact with them, he exposed their lack of purpose.

They saw in him something they wanted. They saw a purpose. A reason. They were tired of living with no aspiration. They were willing to embrace an opportunity to live for something bigger than themselves. They wanted something worth living for. Eventually it would become a cause worth dying for.

They Saw Excitement

They had been living day after day in a routine. This rut had entrenched them in boredom and enslaved them. Every day was the same. Nothing was new. Then they met Jesus.

They had not been out looking for something to spice up their life because they did not know such a thing existed. But the moment they saw Jesus, they had hope for an exciting future. They probably knew it would be difficult, but they were willing to take the tough times along with the good because the anticipation of what they would see, do, and hear overwhelmed them.

When Jesus made eye contact with them, he exposed their lack of purpose.

Jesus' tone of voice convinced them of his love and enticed them with adventure. While following Jesus, they would see incredible miracles daily. They would hear truths about God preached by one who knew him intimately and personally. They would get to cast out demons and heal the sick themselves. The journey would be difficult on occasion, yet they knew that the joy of getting up every day and the knowledge that excitement was around every corner made the journey worth it.

They wanted to live on the edge.

What about the Others?

I can't help but think about the others who could have chosen to follow Jesus but didn't.

When Jesus was walking along the shore, he did not call out the four by name. He saw a group of men who were all loved by the Father, and he invited all of them to follow. The Bible doesn't record how many people were around, but we know there were at least a few other men, the hired men and the father of James and John. Why didn't they follow Jesus?

They must have seen something different than Andrew, Peter, James, and John. They must not have seen enough excitement or purpose to make them want to leave the shore. Evidently they did not see a future; they were content with the future that they were building for themselves.

I believe any of these men could have been included in what Jesus was going to do because I know that he will pour his life into anyone that chooses to follow him. Maybe they thought Jesus was "interesting," but they didn't think he was worth following. Maybe their reputation and image was stronger than their desire to be associated with Jesus. Possibly they wanted to be known as hard-working fishermen instead of humble and serving disciples.

Same Scenario, Different Century

Whatever the reason, these men missed out just like many people today. There are extremes—those who ignore the call and those who embrace it.

All across this world people are surrendering their hearts to Christ and following him because they see in him the one who can change their lives. In Jesus, they see a future that is bright. They see a love that is perfect and will never leave them, even in difficult times. Many people are willing to give up their identity because they see a better one in Jesus. People see the abundant life that only comes from knowing, walking with, and following Jesus.

Even today Jesus walks past individuals and calls out to them. When they see who Jesus is and what he longs to do in their lives, they have no choice but to follow him. "Immediately" or "without hesitation," people are leaving their old lives and following Christ, yet some by not saying "yes" are saying "no."

What you see when you look at Jesus will determine what you do with him.

Reality Check

- How do you think your future has changed as a result of choosing to follow Jesus?

- Does Jesus' love make all of the other loves you have known seem less significant? How does Jesus' love comfort you?

- What is your identity tied up in? Do you have problems trusting God with your identity and reputation? If so, why?

- Do you feel like your life is filled with purpose? What practical steps can you take to give your life a purpose boost?

- Do you consider your relationship with God exciting or do you see it as boring? If boring, what actions does God want you to do that will add excitement to your relationship with him?

God, thank you *for loving me and inviting me to walk with you. Thank you for giving me a future and a purpose. I ask that you shape my identity and direct my life in every way possible. Never let me forget that you are my source of joy and you are what fulfills me. I ask that you help me to see you as you truly are, so that I will not hold anything back from you. This day, I choose to follow you. I look forward to our journey together as I get to know you more and have the privilege of serving you. I am yours. Amen.*

2

God is Waiting

"Come to me, all you who are weary and burdened, and I will give you rest."

MATTHEW 11:28

"Zuriel, come along. It is time."

Zuriel's father was calling him to join the family outside their tent. Several times a week their whole community would line the pathways in front of their tents as Moses would make his way to the tent of meeting. The process used to excite Zuriel, but by now it had become routine.

It wasn't long ago that the thought of Moses spending time in the presence of God created a sense of wonder. No more. It had been several years since it had been anything but an exercise in tradition.

"Where are you, boy?" his father called again. "The whole family is waiting on you. He is almost here."

Annoyed at the inconvenience, he left what he was doing and joined his father, mother, and two brothers outside their home. His younger siblings were pushing each other until Dad broke it up and told them to look respectable. The family had to look good as Moses passed.

As was the custom, every home in the community emptied as families lined the corridor of tents. The people looked forward to the times when Moses would leave the camp to visit the tent of meeting. On those occasions everyone would participate. Not one person was left inside. With anticipation they would wait for Moses to enter because this was when the presence of the Lord would appear in the visible form of a cloud resting on this unique tent.

Around the corner he finally came, with his usual group of escorts. The security was in place, and his advisors were walking beside him, but there was one that caught Zuriel's eye. A young man about the same age as Zuriel was walking right beside Moses. Quietly Zuriel watched as the group paraded past his family, but as soon as they were out of range, Zuriel quickly turned to ask his father who the young man was. "Why, that is Joshua; he is being trained to take over when Moses retires," answered his father.

"Take over?" he questioned in his mind. "How can someone that young be in charge of this entire nation?" He was skeptical, yet intrigued. He decided to observe and try to find out more about this future leader.

The first thing Zuriel noticed about Joshua was that he had special privileges. As they neared the entrance to the tent, everyone in Moses' entourage began to fan out—

everyone, that is, except for Joshua. He was the only advisor who accompanied Moses into the tent of meeting.

Zuriel watched to see what would happen next. As always, God showed up. The cloud fell and the people began to worship. Zuriel's imagination ran wild as he wondered what Moses and Joshua were doing and seeing inside the tent.

After an hour or so, Zuriel started to lose interest. But his curiosity was piqued again as he noticed movement around the tent. All the soldiers that escorted Moses to the tent began to form the ranks and his advisors returned to the front of the tent from where they had been resting. Just a few seconds later Moses appeared from the tent and began his short walk back into the camp. But where was Joshua? He was not with Moses.

The crowds began to clear as everyone entered their tents or went about their business. Children began to run and play again. Mothers began to prepare the evening meal, and fathers were seen checking their tents for leaks or their cords to make sure they were tight. Everyone left their perch outside their tent—except Zuriel. He wasn't going to leave until he discovered the whereabouts and the "what-abouts" of the mysterious Joshua.

For another forty-five minutes he waited. Without any commotion or fanfare, Joshua exited the tent. Not one other person noticed as he slowly walked back into camp.

Zuriel had to know. He tried to convince himself not to ask the question, but as Joshua came near, his curiosity got the better of him. He had always wanted to know, but now that someone his own age had experienced it, the questions burned all the more intensely within him. "Hey," he called to Joshua as he walked by, "what is it like in there?"

Joshua stopped and looked over at the curious young man. With a light-hearted, yet serious look in his eyes, he answered, "Why not go find out for yourself?" Joshua looked back at the tent of meeting with a look that drew Zuriel's gaze also. However, the sight he had seen hundreds of times before looked different. Instead of looking from a distance, he was considering going in himself. He wanted to take his turn in the tent of meeting.

The Tent of Meeting

> Now Moses used to take a tent and pitch it outside the camp some distance away, calling it the "tent of meeting." Anyone inquiring of the Lord would go to the tent of meeting outside the camp. And whenever Moses went out to the tent, all the people rose and stood at the entrances to their tents, watching Moses until he entered the tent. As Moses went into the tent, the pillar of cloud would come down and stay at the entrance, while the Lord spoke with Moses. Whenever the people saw the pillar of cloud standing at the entrance to the tent, they all stood and worshiped, each at the entrance to his tent. The Lord would speak to Moses face to face, as a man speaks with his friend. Then Moses would return to the camp, but his young aide Joshua son of Nun did not leave the tent.
>
> Exodus 33:7–11

In Exodus 33:7–11 the Bible tells us about the tent that Moses established and the purposes behind it. In this short passage we read about four principles that created one of the most exciting opportunities ever known to any living person. The four principles are these:

1. Anyone can go.
2. God's presence will show up.
3. Intimate communication will take place.
4. You can stay as long as you want.

These are the four principles that still apply today and will radically affect the life of anyone who takes his or her turn in the "tent of meeting." The "tent of meeting" is no longer a place but an attitude. It is an aggressive posture and a pursuit. The people that enter into this very special and vital tent relationship with God are the ones who are learning to delight themselves in him (Psalms 37:4), meditate upon his word (Psalms 1), and passionately seek him (Matthew 6:33).

By turning your heart and attention to God, you are entering into a place of intimate communication with God and vibrant communion. Whenever you shut out the world's noises to concentrate on Christ's character, you are there. Whenever his children sneak away to linger with God, his presence, peace, joy, and abundant blessing are with them.

Anyone Can Go

In verse 7 the Bible declared that "anyone inquiring of the Lord" could go into the tent of meeting. The invitation was not limited to ministers and preachers. There were no requirements concerning age or spiritual maturity. The promise simply said anyone who wanted to go, could go.

I wonder, however, how many people never took their turn in Moses' day. I wonder how many people never take the opportunity to meet with God today. I picture a lot of people filing out of their homes to line the corridor of tents as Moses passed and entered the tent. I see many of them getting excited and praising God that their spiritual leader was getting the opportunity to meet with God, *but how many of them never took the opportunity themselves?*

The incredible thing about our God is that he offers an open invitation for any who want to meet with him. His door is always open, and he does not discriminate. If you want to go in, he will welcome you.

God's Presence Will Show Up

When Moses went in, God met him there. That sounds very similar to a promise God made to us in the passage that says, "If we come near to him, he will come near to us"

(James 4:8a). If we make the effort to seek God, God will allow us to experience his presence. He will not turn us away.

When I take the time to separate myself from all the chaos of this world, God comes and meets with me. I know he will do the same for you.

Intimate Communication Will Take Place

"The Lord would speak to Moses face to face, as a man speaks with his friend." Wow, what an incredible relationship Moses had with God. "Face to Face." God and man talking as friends.

This is the kind of awesome communication that you will experience when you enter into the tent. Not one-way communication, but two-way conversation where you share with him and he shares with you. In that kind of relationship, you can talk about everything that matters and things that don't matter. You can share important things, and just by sharing mundane things you make them important. Intense communication between friends—it happens in the tent.

The incredible thing about our God is that he offers an open invitation for any who want to meet with him.

You Can Stay As Long As You Want

In typical relationships you can wear out your welcome. You can stay so long that the person you are visiting gets tired of you and wants space. This does not happen when you are in a "tent relationship" with God. According to verse 11, Joshua stayed until he wanted to leave. God did not kick him out, and he was free to stay longer than his leader, Moses. He stayed longer, prayed hard, and left fulfilled in his relationship with the Lord.

God is waiting for you to long for his presence so much that you will stay a little bit longer than you had intended. He wants you to come daily into his presence and not leave until you have touched his heart.

Time for the Tent

There you go. Those are the principles that established the tent of meeting. They worked way back in Joshua's day, and they work today. Your first step toward Christ is salvation. Your second step is to set aside some "tent time." This is when your relationship with Christ will begin to grow. It is in the tent that you will discover who he is, who you are, and what he has set you apart for. When you are there, you will meet him one on one, and when you leave, you will be familiar enough with his voice to hear him in the midst of a confusing world.

Calling YOU into the Tent

There's a famous street in Tijuana, Mexico. It's called Revolution Street and it's famous for two reasons. Tourists cross the border between Tijuana and San Diego, California, by the millions every year for the purpose of (1) shopping and (2) partying.

I have been there several times, and I find it interesting that every store and club spends money to employ people for the simple purpose of attracting people to the bargains inside their establishments. You cannot walk down this street without one of these "callers" trying to convince you that their store or club is the place you need to go to spend your time and money. These people are persistent and loud as they call out for your attention. If you take the time to listen to their pleas, you will begin to believe that their merchandise really is better than the store down the street. You will be convinced that their prices are better than in others. The "callers" are strategically placed, and they intentionally work to get your attention.

I hope that God will use the information that has been strategically, intentionally, and prayerfully placed in this chapter to call you into the tent of meeting. As with the callers on Revolution Street, this message is urgent. God wants you to join him inside.

What Happens in the Tent?

The things God will do in your life as you take time to meet with him are limitless. However, it is good to know how you should approach him. Because you are still reading and haven't already put this book on the shelf, I assume that you want to develop your times with the Lord into something that is beneficial and life changing. Although you have a strong desire to meet with God, you may not know exactly how to get started or how to get the most benefit out of your times with the Lord. Below you'll find some information about what to do once you commit to take time in the tent with the Lord.

As you begin to spend time with the Lord, you should include three things in your times with God. They are worship, Bible reading, and prayer. Although you may have known for some time that these things are beneficial to your spiritual growth, let's look specifically at how you can include these things in your times with God.

Worship

Worship is always easier in a crowd; people tend to love to worship when the band sounds good and the congregational setting is energetic and fun. However, people often neglect worship when they are alone with God, and they shouldn't. Worship should be a major component of your time alone with the Lord.

Your times of isolation with God should include sweet times of worship when you open up your heart to him. You can do this using a CD of worship music. You can spend some time reading, meditating on, and pondering the Psalms, or you can tell God in your own words how much he means to you. Worship is an attitude. It doesn't have to include music, although it can if you like. However, it does have to be a part of your relationship with God.

As you begin to add worship into your daily times with God, find out which way works best for you. You may need to begin by using music and singing along with another person's words and style of worship. As you practice worshiping, you will discover that you become a better worshiper.

Worship is not an activity, it is an attitude and it becomes a lifestyle. Work to develop this more within your relationship with God.

Read the Bible

I can still remember my first Bible. It was more of a symbol than anything else. I didn't read it much, and when I did, I would get lost. As a young teenager of fourteen, I thought the Bible was boring. Although I loved God and wanted desperately to walk closely with him, I neglected his gift of Scripture because my perception was wrong.

However, around that time I began to read the Bible because a youth pastor told me that in it lay the key to my Christian growth. I made a commitment to invest my time and energy into reading, studying, memorizing, and understanding the words that were "God breathed" (2 Timothy 3:16).

A remarkable thing happened. Not only did I learn to discipline myself and stay consistent in my reading, but I fell in love with the Bible. It fascinated me with stories of war, enticed me with characters so daring and committed that they were willing to give their lives for their cause, and challenged me by speaking directly into my everyday life. The more I read, the more the blinders came off. Instead of avoiding it, or just getting through it, I began to savor it.

If you want to know who God is, what he thinks about, and who he wants you to be, begin reading the greatest book ever written—the Bible.

The Bible was no longer a symbol. It was not a duty any more. It had become a source of hope and joy to me. And it became a tool that God used to direct me, shape me, and build in me the convictions, passions, and heart that he desired for me to have.

Looking back, I realize it was my love for the Bible and daily involvement in it that helped me become the person God wanted me to be. If I had not invested time and energy in reading it, I am not sure who I would be today.

That is why it is imperative that you read the Bible—not only for what it will do for your mind and intellect, but also for what it will do for your heart. If you want to know who God is, what he thinks about, and who he wants you to be, begin reading the greatest book ever written—the Bible. Pick it up daily and read it with anticipation.

Pray Like You Have Never Prayed Before

The third discipline that I believe needs to be included in your times alone with God is the discipline of prayer. However, I do not want you to pray the average prayer. I want God to teach you how to touch heaven and hear the Lord's voice.

Prayer that gets God's attention does not consist of you always talking and him always listening. You need to get a glimpse of what true prayer is. You see, God is wanting to teach you about who he is, who you are, and how the two of you are supposed to work together to accomplish great things for the kingdom of God.

Prayer is not about what you want but what he wants. You shouldn't always tell him what you are worried about, you should take time to hear what he is concerned about. That is the kind of prayer that makes the relationship that you build with God in the tent of meeting different from the average Christian's. It is this kind of communication that will allow God to trust you with things that he truly cares about.

When you pray, take time to:

1. Worship him. We have already talked about this, but do not overlook the importance of this step. It is in this step that you begin to have the right focus so the rest of the time that you spend with him will be sweet. When you worship him, you begin to see him as he is; he is able to tackle any obstacle or move any mountain. The rest of your time with God will benefit greatly if you take time to remember and verbalize his greatness (Psalm 103).

2. Confess. Don't overlook your problems and the sins that seem to dominate your life. Confess them to the Lord and ask him for strength to overcome them (1 John 1:9; 2 Corinthians 12:9–10).
3. Reflect. Ask the Lord to show you where you may be in danger of falling into sin. Ask him to reveal to you any areas where he is not pleased with you. Psalm 139:23–24 says, "Search me, O God, and know my heart; test me and know my anxious thoughts. See if there is any offensive way in me, and lead me in the way everlasting." Pray that prayer and allow God to show you your faults not just in actions, but in attitudes and thoughts as well.
4. Thank him. One of the best tools that you will have as you try to strengthen your relationship with God every day is a good memory. Take time each day to remember what he has done for you in the past. If you remember what he did for you yesterday or a week ago, it will keep you focused on his goodness and give you the faith you need to face a difficulty tomorrow (Philippians 4:6).
5. Listen. You will find that God wants to share his heart with you. He is waiting for you to listen so he can tell you what he cares about. Take time to ask him what he is burdened over and listen.
6. Ask. The Bible makes it clear that it is okay for us to "make petitions" (Philippians 4:6). There are things that concern us or that we want to see happen that we are allowed and even encouraged to share with him. He is waiting and he will listen. The problem that we have is not that we forget to ask him for what concerns us, but that we neglect all the other things. Don't forget all of the other components to healthy prayer, but don't neglect talking with God about your needs, wants, or desires either.

7. Share your heart. For some reason we have made prayer into a mechanical thing. We seem to think we have a ration of words with which to communicate to God, and we don't want to use them up talking about less important things like feelings. However, the best way that I have found to receive comfort is to express my true feelings to the Lord. If you are dealing with feelings of loneliness or inadequacy, he already knows, but you will begin to feel a release from those very real and strong emotions if you sit in his presence and talk with him about how you are feeling. I encourage you to talk with God about anything that concerns you. Don't wait for a crisis to turn to God.

An Incredible Opportunity

I hope you understand by now that you have been given the opportunity to have a "tent of meeting" every day. God is waiting for you to take your turn inside the tent. Not only do I hope and pray that you know he is waiting for you, I also pray that you are starting to see the need to carve out time each day to spend with him. I trust that God is speaking to you and you are beginning to have a desire to know God in an intimate way.

When and Where?

Many great ideas have gone unnoticed because they were not followed up with action. For this reason I want you to take some time to decide how you will apply the principles you have just read. If you believe God is calling you into his tent, you can't neglect it. You must make a plan of action. You must answer two questions. When and Where?

If you wait for time alone with God to be convenient, you will never take time to get to know him. There will always be something else calling for your attention. Something else will seem more important at the moment. So, before you go any further, decide where you are going to set up your tent. Now determine when. Are you going to take time in the morning, or are you going to set aside time in the afternoon?

Possibly you are thinking about the time you waste in front of the TV right before you go to bed at night. Maybe you are going to do what I did and take some time in the morning and some time in the evening. Whatever you decide, stick to it. Spending time must be a priority if you are going to live this new life of discovery with God.

Zuriel Took His Turn

After Joshua was out of sight, Zuriel continued looking at the tent of meeting. His curiosity was aroused, and he had to know. Slowly he walked toward the tent, but no one noticed. He did not draw a crowd like Moses had, but he was captivated. Something about the fact that God would meet with him as he had with Moses made him continue.

As he reached for the tent flap, his anticipation peaked. He didn't know what to expect, but he knew he would never be the same. The tent of meeting was no longer an exercise in tradition, it was his opportunity to experience God. He no longer had to settle for merely hearing about God in services and from his parents; now it was his turn to discover God.

Timidly, yet with excitement in his heart, Zuriel entered the tent. His relationship with God was about to take off.

Reality Check

- Have you had a habit of taking time to meet with God in the past? Have you been one of those who worshiped from a distance, but never took your turn? You ready to change that?

- Which of the four points from Exodus 33:7–11 meant the most to you? Why?

- This chapter lists three things you should be doing in God's presence. Is there one that you neglect more than the others? Is there one that you enjoy more than the others? Why?

- Which of the components of prayer that was listed challenged you the most? Why?

- Which one challenged you the least? Why?

Father God, *I don't only want to know about you. I want to know who you are. I will no longer be satisfied worshiping you from a distance; I commit to come close. Teach me how to spend time with you. Show me how to worship you even in the everyday moments of life. Teach me how to pray so that I am not merely sharing with you my needs, but I am hearing your heart. Teach me how to hear your voice, enjoy your presence, and understand your Word. I accept your invitation to come near to you. I love you. I pray in the name of Jesus. Amen.*

3

Sit Before Serving

"Christianity has not been tried and found wanting. It has been found difficult and left untried."

G. K. CHESTERTON

I met him at a youth camp this past summer. The first thing I noticed about him was his overwhelming zeal. Everything he did, he did with energy. Every time he spoke (especially about the Lord), he was loud. Every movement was impossible to ignore. When he prayed, he shook heaven and inspired the people around him. I knew it from the moment that I saw him. There was a calling on his life.

God had his hand on Jonathan. The Spirit of God had given him a boldness to say what he felt. And somewhere along the way, he had developed a presence about him that made everybody listen with anticipation and watch in awe.

He was a leader among leaders. At this particular camp he was more of a spiritual influence than many of the youth leaders, and he was only sixteen. People went to him for counsel, and they approached him for prayer.

In some situations there even seemed to be mild cases of hero worship. He drew more people in the cafeteria than anyone else. People were flocking to him just to spend time with him because they respected his spiritual insight and his charismatic personality.

After having been at the camp for three days, I had begun to build a healthy relationship with Jonathan. We started talking for a few minutes whenever we could between activities and services. However, these five-minute sessions weren't enough; he wanted more time with me. I agreed to get up early on the fourth day of the camp and meet him inside the cafeteria for a heart to heart.

As I went to bed that night, I was praying for the young people at the camp. That's when my mind rested on Jonathan, and God began to give me a glimpse into his heart.

I saw him as a young man with pure motives. However, something in his life was slightly backwards. Jonathan loved to serve, but he was constantly giving of himself and not receiving anything from the Lord. He was representing Christ to all of his peers, but he had forgotten to take time to know the one he was representing.

That night, I sensed a burden that God had for Jonathan. The Lord's desire was not to keep pushing him into leadership roles and forcing him to serve constantly; God wanted to minister directly to Jonathan. God wanted to comfort him and encourage him. God's desire was not to make sure Jonathan did a lot for the kingdom of God, his first desire was to spend time with his child.

I fell asleep with a burden on my heart for Jonathan, praying that he would be open to the words I needed to speak to him the next morning.

Morning came. I jumped out of my sleeping bag and got ready for my day. Although a few hours had passed since I had been praying for Jonathan, I still had a very real sense that God wanted to draw his child into a more intimate relationship. The time came for me to leave my cabin and walk to the cafeteria. The entire way I prayed that the Lord would give me the words to speak to Jonathan, because I knew deep down that God's heart was reaching out to this young man.

As I expected him to be, Jonathan was on time. Joining him at the table that he already occupied, I told him I had been praying for him. I began to share with him about the conversation I had with God the night before. He was very open.

When I finished and asked him what he thought of what I had just said, he became very somber. He quietly told me that he knew I was right. He was running on empty spiritually and serving out of routine. He was dry and he didn't know how to tap into God's presence that had once been so real to him.

As I talked with him for several minutes, I saw a young man who represented many young people I know. Their burning desire is to make the Lord known. They want to serve him. They want their generation to know the incredible love that Jesus offers them, yet they have neglected getting to know him themselves. There are many teenagers today who have wanted to "do for God," but they have forgotten how to "be with him."

In life, there is sometimes an order to things. If you want to make God known, you must first get to know him yourself. God's desire is that you would spend time with him before you spend time serving him. Jesus modeled this with his disciples even in the midst of a busy season of ministry.

He invited them, saying, "Come away with me by yourselves to a quiet place and get some rest" (Mark 6:31). He knew that in the hectic schedules of life, we can grow spiritually dry. But in a vital relationship with our Creator we get refreshed.

Your first responsibility and the thing that will determine your success in terms of serving God is how well you know him.

God's calling on your life is specific. He formed you for a specific purpose (Jeremiah 29:11) and he knew you before you were formed (Psalm 139:13–16). Your life has a destiny. However, your first responsibility and the thing that will determine your success in terms of serving God is how well you know him.

Mary and Martha

When Jesus came to her house, Martha was busy. She was preparing the food, cleaning (so as to not be embarrassed), and doing the things that a good hostess should do. Her motives were pure and her intentions honorable. However, she neglected something very important.

Mary was not concerned with service; she was consumed by Jesus. His teaching and his presence captivated her. She gave her attention to every sentence that came from his mouth. She knew that a time was coming when she would be serving him, but she didn't want to miss a chance to sit at his feet and be with him. She lived for these moments.

Martha and Mary were two sisters who both loved the Lord dearly yet took very different approaches to pleasing him. One served while the other sat. One prepared while the other listened. One was hard at work trying to please him while the other was caught up with getting to know Jesus.

Martha was frustrated because she was falling behind. (People whose only goal is to serve never seem to get caught up; they always see more that needs to be done.) The Bible says in verse 40 of chapter 10 of Luke that she was "distracted by all of the preparations that had to be made." The word "distracted" indicates there was something more worthy of her attention than her chores.

However, Martha's perspective was skewed. She did not see the open spot on the floor right next to Jesus that he had reserved for her; she only saw the duties that she needed to perform. She wanted sympathy, and she wanted help.

She asked Jesus, "Lord, don't you care that my sister has left me to do the work all by myself? Tell her to help me!"

Jesus had noticed the energy that Martha was using to run around the house doing things, and he noticed her frustration. But when she finally made her request, it gave him permission to show her a proper perspective. "Martha, Martha, you are worried and upset about many things, *but only one thing is needed. Mary has chosen what is better,* and it will not be taken away from her" (the italics are mine).

Jesus did not say serving was a wrong thing to do, but he longed to minister to Martha before she started serving. He called her back to the right priorities. "Only one thing is needed. Mary has chosen what is better."

That is where the story ends in Scripture, but in real life there had to be more. In that moment and with those words, Jesus was not rebuking a servant; he was wooing a child of the Father. He wasn't going to crush her for serving, he was going to invite her to come, sit, and share.

I wonder what her response was. Do you think she took him up on his offer?

I think she did, but I think it was difficult for her. When you have a habit of serving, sitting is not easy for you. However, it is the time you spend with your Lord that keeps you from getting frustrated in service and enables you to keep a good attitude and not burn out. Once the Lord got her to sit down, I believe he had to teach her to concentrate on him and not on the food that was waiting in the kitchen. He wanted Martha to know him, and then she would be called to serve him.

To Know Him and Make Him Known

Are you like Jonathan? Do you see yourself in Martha? Are you so concerned with what you are doing for the Lord that you are neglecting spending time with him? Are you serving constantly? Are your "sitting sessions" becoming more and more infrequent?

I pray that as you read this book, you will hear the Lord calling you to sit down at his feet and listen to him. He wants you to know him. Through these pages he wants to teach you how to build intimacy and find encouragement. As he invites you to know him more intimately, you will discover his love and comfort. In return, the relationship that you have with him will empower you to serve him more effectively.

Reality Check

- Do you spend more time getting to know God or serving him? Is this out of balance in your life?

- Is God calling you into a more intimate walk with himself? If so, how are you going to develop this?

- Do you get frustrated in your walk with God? What does the story about Martha teach you about frustration?

- What obstacles prevent you from spending more time with God?

Father, I am so grateful *that you want me to sit with you and listen to you before I go out into the world and serve you. I acknowledge my tendencies to neglect these times with you. However, I ask that you would teach me just how to do that. When I begin to get too preoccupied with things and I forget you are waiting for me to spend time with you, remind me. If I begin to perform my faith to impress people, help me to get back to the basics and return to the place where you convince me how much you love me. I need you more than anything else. May I never forget that. Amen.*

4

Chosen

"Only he who can see the invisible can do the impossible."
Frank Gaines

Once again God had chosen an unlikely man to work for him. No one would have chosen Saul of Tarsus as the one to champion the causes and message of Jesus Christ. After all, Saul didn't even believe his claims.

At the time God chose to call him into ministry, Saul was occupied full-time persecuting the Christians. He was there giving his approval when the angry mob decided to kill Stephen for preaching Christ. He had gone to the proper authorities to get legal documents giving him permission to torment followers of Jesus in Damascus. Not only was siding with Christ unthinkable to Saul, he wanted to wipe Christ and his followers out.

That's when God tapped on his shoulder.

I am not sure if we will ever understand why God chose him. However, we can learn a great deal about how God changed Saul to Paul. God transformed him from someone who despised the Lord to someone who could be trusted with this incredible responsibility. If we want to be effective ambassadors for the Lord, our journey will be similar to Paul's in many ways.

The Conversion

In what he thought to be a righteous rage, Saul was headed toward Damascus (Acts 9). He had received word that the followers of Christ were proselytizing and he had taken it upon himself to point out the error of their ways. He was going to bring an end to their zealous efforts by being overly zealous himself.

That's when his theology changed. He met Jesus. He was not looking for him. He was convinced that Jesus was dead. All that talk about him being raised from the dead was nonsense—superstition at best, a calculated hoax at worst.

He wasn't looking for Jesus, but Jesus was looking for him. He didn't recognize his need for a savior, but the Savior of the world wanted Saul.

A bright light shone. He fell to the ground and had a short conversation with the Lord. This dialogue changed the course of his life. Everything he had scheduled for his future was now futile.

Paul was blind for three days after this rendezvous, so his companions led him to Damascus. Everything he had known and lived for was now meaningless. He had met the Messiah, and he was a new man. He joined the cause.

Changing Saul into Paul

He was Saul before he met Christ and shortly after his name became Paul. His name change marked a change in direction, calling, and purpose.

The only cause Saul had ever known was to defend tradition, but now God was calling him to do two things: to know God and to make God known.

On the road to Damascus Saul met Jesus. Before his life was over, he would tell his story and preach the gospel through letters and in person to more people than anyone before or since. However, he did not immediately go from the Damascus road experience to being an expert preacher. He began a lifelong journey of knowing him.

Ananias's Message

Paul was God's chosen messenger to the world, but Ananias was God's messenger to Paul. After the Lord convinced Ananias that Paul was waiting on him, he headed over to where the future apostle was staying. His first job was to restore his sight. As things like scales fell off his natural eyes, some added instruction from Ananias changed the way Paul saw God and approached him spiritually.

Ananias said, "The God of our fathers has chosen you to know his will and to see the Righteous One and to hear words from his mouth. You will be his witness to all men of what you have seen and heard" (Acts 22:14–15). These two sentences affected the way Paul built his relationship with God. Let me explain.

"The God of Our Fathers Has Chosen You"

The first thing Paul needed to understand was that God chose him. This is something all Christians need to understand. Your parents did not choose you to be a Christian,

God did. You are not a Christian because that is all you have ever known, because you go to a youth group, or because you attend a Christian school. *God chose you.* While you were still in the womb, God handpicked you. Before you breathed your first breath, he decided he wanted you.

Why?

To start a revolution? Well, that may be a result of your life, but that is not the main reason he chose you.

Did he choose you to bring revival to your church or school? Again, you may, but that is not what he chose you for.

He chose you so that you could know him. The way you build a relationship with him is the same way Saul did. Ananias told Saul God chose him to do three things: know his will, see the Righteous One, and hear words from his mouth.

"Know His Will"

If one of your heroes knocked on your door and asked you for a few minutes, you would definitely give it to him or her. Maybe you are an athlete and one of the all-time best at your sport wanted to take a few minutes to share some things with you. Would you hesitate? We would never think about saying no to our heroes, yet many people ignore God.

Every day he knocks on your door and asks you for some time. Even though you can't see him, he wants to sit down with you and talk to you about his will. He will whisper in your ear what he is thinking, what he is planning. He will share strategies for your school. God will give you an outline for your life.

Think about it. God will take time to let you know his will—for your future, your church, anything and everything.

The problem is many people refuse to take time to listen.

"See the Righteous One"

When you look into the face of the world, what do you see? Hatred, anger, rage? You see violence in schools, immorality in the streets, and petty images in the media. Many heroes are not worth respecting and many goals are not worth achieving. If you spend all of your time looking at the world, you will be demoralized, hopeless, and frustrated.

God wants to speak directly to you.

God has chosen you to see the Righteous One. If you take time to sit down and look at the Lord, what will you see? You will gaze into the face of perfection. He is the exact opposite of what you see in the world.

When you spend hours daily looking at hate, you need to balance it with love. When looking into the eyes of Christ, you will see love—the perfect kind of love that chases away your doubts, fears, and sins.

You will see joy—unadulterated delight.

You will see peace—a peace that surpasses all understanding and goes beyond all circumstances.

Patience, kindness, goodness, faithfulness, gentleness, and self-control—these are what you will find when you look into the character of Christ.

"Hear Words from His Mouth"

God wants to speak directly to you. Although you may sit under a gifted leader and have great teachers in your church, it is more exciting when you hear wisdom from God himself. He chose you to be a hearer of his words. He handpicked you to receive his wisdom, direction, and insights so that you can be shaped and molded by them.

Then you will be his witness to everyone of what you have seen and heard.

After you know his will, see him, and hear what he has to say, you will be an effective witness. Many Christians try to be an effective witness, but they never take time to listen to him and see him.

The most effective ambassadors will be the ones who carve out time to spend in solitude with God. Only the ones who embrace the opportunities to know him this intimately will change the world.

What Paul Did

God handpicked Paul to preach. He was appointed an apostle and a herald, yet it was not an instant change. Ananias came and shared the plan that would change him, yet it was up to Paul to follow through with the plan. God took the initiative, but Paul had to be willing to take the time.

I can't tell you what God's plan for you is in regard to impacting the world, but I can tell you he wants you to know his will, see him, and hear him. If you do, you will be effective at whatever he calls you to do. If you say no, you will never reach your potential.

It was the key for Paul, and it will be the key for you also.

Reality Check

- Do you believe "God chose you" to have a radical relationship with him? Are you convinced that he singled you out simply so that he could reveal himself to you? How will this affect the way that you approach your devotional life?

* Romans 12:2 says that you can "test and approve what God's will is—his good, pleasing, and perfect will." How does it make you feel to know he wants you "to know his will"?

* For what specific areas would you like to understand his will?

* If you take time to pray, you can see his face and sense his presence. Have you ever felt like you connected with God in this way? In your quiet times do you feel like you have been able to get a glimpse of his goodness and love?

God, thank you *for choosing me. You do speak to me and want me to hear your voice. Help me to recognize you when you are trying to teach, lead, or direct me. I desperately want to know you and your will. I will sit and listen, and when you speak I will respond. I love you and I thank you that you love me. In the great name of Jesus, I pray. Amen.*

5

Spitting Image

"You are what you are—but that's not all that you are. You are what you are, but you are not yet what you will be."
JOHN ORTBERG

She hung on every word. You could see in her eyes an admiration that went way beyond appreciation. This man captivated her. He was her dad and he meant the world to her.

As a little child, she loved to sit in his lap and whisper secrets in his ear. Some days he would tickle her until her stomach hurt from laughing, while other days he would hoist her onto his shoulders and walk over to the park to play. Their time together was plentiful and vibrant as they shared laughs, smiles, whispers, and hugs.

They had so many memories together, and every day they would add to their collection. Playing Barbies in the playroom, drinking tea with their pinkies extended, coloring pictures of animals—all these activities and others filled many pages in their mental photo album.

As she grew into her teens, she still loved her dad, but she enjoyed different things about him. Instead of always playing, she just wanted to be near him. She loved to watch him, listen to him, and she wanted to know what he thought about everything.

Whether they were watching a baseball game together, grabbing a cup of coffee at the corner shop, or catching a movie on the weekend, their times together were special. They talked about everything important and many things that were not very important. The older she got, the less she talked and the more she listened.

An Amazing Discovery

As she reached her twenties, she remained close to her family and especially to her father, although she was living three hours away from home. She would visit whenever she could, and a well-timed call would get her through some confusing and difficult times.

Then it happened. One day while she was out shopping for groceries with her roommate, she heard her father's words. She stopped in the aisle as she realized she had just repeated something he told her in the past. Standing with a glazed look on her face, she realized for the first time that in many ways she was just like her father.

When her roommate saw the stunned look on her face, she asked what was wrong. Puzzled look still intact, she responded, "I'm just like my dad!"

Her friend responded, "You are the *spitting image* of your dad."

For hours she quietly pondered this new realization. Up to this point she had never analyzed herself and evaluated who she was. But as she lay in bed that night, she couldn't sleep. She understood for the first time that she was very similar to her dad in many ways.

She asked herself, "How did this happen? When and why did I become that much like my father?"

Although she fell asleep without any firm answers, she was smiling. As her thoughts became cloudy, she was pleased to know noticeable traces of her father were within her.

How Did This Happen?

How did the father show up in his daughter? Was it a genetic transference or something else? The time they spent together was the mechanism that transferred the father's attributes to his daughter and in many ways helped her become a replica of the one she had admired since birth. Each of them was intertwined with the other.

Over the years his opinions shaped hers. Her personality became a reflection of his. His philosophy of life and his disposition began to resonate through her, and her makeup became almost identical to his.

Taking On His Attributes

Just as this daughter discovered she had become like her father in many ways, so children of God begin to resemble their heavenly Father as they grow up in and with him. Time spent with him is the mechanism by which you will begin to notice transformation within you. As you faithfully take time to get to know God, you will look like him in many ways.

Your Worldview Will Begin to Change

It was the summer of 1990 and although I was one of two leaders on this trip, this was my first missions experience. We were young youth pastors with a lot of energy and not much experience, but we were taking forty teenagers into Mexico. The majority of them had never been out of the country.

Traveling on a slow bus that had given us problems ever since we left Colorado, we were heading through San Diego. The colors were vibrant and the scenery was beautiful. Everywhere we looked we saw testimonies of wealth displayed in huge homes and expensive cars.

We rode along, amazed at the sights, not knowing that in just a few minutes we would be amazed for the exact opposite reasons. Instead of being caught off guard by the abundance, we were going to be floored by the poverty.

Just a few miles outside the city limits of San Diego is the U.S.-Mexican border. Mike, the other youth pastor, and I decided we should get our young people praying. Approaching the border, we outlawed talking on the bus and told everyone to pray quietly.

The border patrol didn't give us any trouble, and we crossed over easily. Immediately we noticed a change. Just a few miles back we had witnessed the comfort and extravagance of the United States; now we were face to face with poverty that most of us had never seen before.

Instead of expensive homes just off the freeway, we saw people sitting next to cardboard boxes. That is what they called home. The cars did not look good either. They were sputtering along potholed roads, paint missing and rust everywhere.

We sat there, soaking in all of the changes, when we began to notice dogs wandering along the road looking half dead and half starved. Several small dogs lay wounded or dead alongside the roads as well. The children were malnourished and dirty. The adults were dressed in yesteryear fashions.

Forty of us sat in complete silence as our hearts broke. We were so used to living our selfish lives and complaining whenever we didn't have the newest fashions, cars, or homes; we never knew anything like this.

Our perspectives began to change. With every person we passed, a little bit of our selfishness died. We wanted to reach out to them. Within a few hours we learned their poverty was not limited to their material possessions, but it was in their spiritual lives as well.

This trip to Mexico started with forty spoiled Americans who had never thought much about things that had no real consequence for anyone other than themselves. It ended with a group who had a heart for the less fortunate, both spiritually and financially. It was a great trip that I have never forgotten. It changed my worldview. In Matthew we read, "Jesus went through all of the towns and villages, teaching in their synagogues, preaching the good news of the kingdom and healing every disease and sickness. When he saw the crowds, he had compassion on them, because they were harassed and helpless, like sheep without a shepherd. Then he said to his disciples, 'The harvest is plentiful but the workers are few. Ask the Lord of the harvest, therefore, to send out workers into his harvest field'" (vv. 9:35–38).

I picture Jesus seeing the hurting, poverty-stricken, and leaderless people and his heart breaking. He knew that before his disciples could impact the world, they must see it the way he did.

I picture him pointing out those without homes, with the physical effects of leprosy, the ones that were outcast, the ones that had been wounded by religious people. As he walked with his disciples, he shared his burdens, and they began to adopt them as their own.

The disciples used to live selfishly, but as they walked with Jesus, they saw what he saw. And it moved them to action. The burdens were too big to ignore and the needs too great to overlook.

Your Convictions Will Become Stronger

Peter was unbelievable. People who were not in the inner circle of Jesus' disciples must have been in awe that this loudmouthed, hot-tempered, over-anxious fisherman was a part of Jesus' pack.

Peter was a man of extremes and opinions that sometimes hit the opposite ends of the spectrum in a matter of seconds. There was the time he told Jesus he was not willing to let the Master wash his feet only to change his mind after Jesus' explanation, declaring that he needed his whole body washed (John 13:8–9). There was the time he said he would go with Jesus anywhere. He declared his commitment was bigger than his fear of death (Matthew 26:33–35). But just a few hours later, he was cursing at someone because she accused him of knowing Jesus (Matthew 26:69–74).

The tell-all sign about Peter's makeup came when Jesus issued a solid rebuke by telling him that Satan was using him to try and distract him from God's plan. "Get behind me, Satan," Jesus said (Matthew 16:23).

Those are four words I would not want to have directed at me by someone I appreciated and respected, yet Peter heard them.

He was rough around the edges in the beginning. He lacked poise, discipline, and discernment. Yet he matured as he meditated on the things he had seen and heard Jesus do and say. And there came a time when Peter's convictions were stronger than his previous outbursts. Somewhere along the way he had learned some lessons and received his Master's philosophy.

He writes, "Therefore, prepare your minds for action; be self-controlled; set your hope fully on the grace to be given you when Jesus Christ is revealed. As obedient children, do not conform to the evil desires you had when you lived in ignorance" (1 Peter 1:13–14).

Had Peter not responded to Jesus' invitation to walk with him and get to know him, he would not have taken on this train of thought. His convictions would not have changed had he not spent time with Jesus. This was not the only place where his convictions became stronger; it was visible in all areas of his life.

Your Attitudes Will Become like His

Only when we spend time with Jesus can we begin to adopt his philosophies and attitudes. When we live apart from him, only hearing about him from the preacher and only experiencing his presence in a church service, we continue to approach life the way we always have. Our selfish nature reigns and our arrogance dominates.

However, by sitting at his feet, reading his word, and embracing his presence, we give him access to our attitudes.

Jordan grew up in my youth ministry. My first memories of him were of him challenging someone to a fight. He was angry and bitter. His past was littered with fights, and he had even spent some time in a psychiatric ward when he went through a period of intense struggling. His family had a history of violence and criminal activity. But Jordan was not anchored to those attitudes and emotions. He wanted to be free.

When he began coming to our church, he met Jesus, and he fell in love. As he began to grow, he realized it was time he began to have daily time alone with God. As he started, something noticeable began to happen in his life. He became softer and more gentle. He was easier to get along with, and he became more patient.

He did not realize his life was changing because he was too close to the situation. But everyone who had known him before was marveling at how God was operating in his life. He was getting a handle on his anger, and other "rough edges" in his life became less abrasive.

I watched Jordan's attitudes become more like those of Jesus. And I've seen this happen with many others too. When people are willing to spend time with God and let his presence invade their lives, their attitudes become more like his.

Your Sin Life Will Decrease

The same way darkness flees when you turn on a light, sin cannot exist in the Lord's presence. God's presence chokes sin, crushes it. If you are living in his presence at his feet, your sin life will decrease.

The same way darkness flees when you turn on a light, sin cannot exist in the Lord's presence.

Growing up, I struggled with many things that other young Christians have wrestled with since the beginning of time. Some of my sins were in my thought life, while others came out of my mouth. Oh, and then there was that problem I had with stealing.

For years I knew that my habits were wrong, but I was unable to break free from these things. However, while in my mid-teens I made a decision to spend time with God every day. Seven days a week, I would read the Bible and spend time in prayer. I was doing all I could to avoid missing any days. I made a conscious effort to know what God thought about things. I tried to love what he loved and hate what he hated.

Within a few months, I looked in the mirror and realized that my sin was decreasing. I began to realize that all of my personal pep talks had done no good, but spending time with God had helped shave off some of my negative habits. I was thrilled with the results. Not only did I get to know who God was, I also had victory in these personal areas.

Every time you draw near to God, you are giving him permission to do surgery on you—to cut off things that are not pleasing to him and to shape you into who he wants you to be.

Family Resemblance

Just today I had lunch with a young man, Shawn, who resembles his father. They don't necessarily look alike, but their actions, words, enunciation, and the way they think are similar. While sitting across from him, my jaw dropped as he gestured during a story just the way his father would have.

Do you think this is genetic? Just because Shawn has the same DNA as his dad, is this why they move alike, think alike, and share many other similarities?

I don't think so! My guess is that if he had been separated from his dad at birth, they would not share many mannerisms at all. Even if he had heard a great deal about his father, this would not have been enough information to wrap their identities together as tightly as they are. The reason they resemble one another is because they have spent countless hours together. They've shared views and opinions. They have hung out together discussing their convictions, and they have shared many stories. It was these moments that made them similar. Because of how much time they spent together, some of the father's peculiarities became second nature to the son.

The same goes for your spiritual life. If you want there to be a family resemblance between you and your heavenly Father, you must spend time with him. If you live separated from him, never taking the time to come into his presence, you will not look much like him. If your only information about God is through someone else, there will not be much resemblance.

On the other hand, if you are faithful to spend time with him, you can become the *spitting image* of your father!

Reality Check

- What is your reaction when you see someone who is less fortunate than you? What do you think when you see someone who is hurting?

- In which areas would you like your convictions to be stronger? How are you similar to or different from the Peter of old who caved in to pressure?

- What attitudes do you have that you know are not pleasing to God? How might spending time in God's presence help change these attitudes?

- What specific things can you do to decrease your sin life? How have you seen sin decrease in your life before?

Father, I want to be *just like you. Teach me to think about the things that you think about, see the things that you see, love that which you love, and hate what you hate. I ask these things because only then will I able to serve you with pure motives. God, as I spend time with you, I pray that you would shape my worldview. May my heart break over the things that break yours. Let my convictions become stronger, and help me overcome the sins in my life. God, give me your attitudes so that I can represent you to this lost world. I pray that as I give you all that I am, you would change me into someone who looks more like you everyday. Let me be consumed with these thoughts, for I believe they are what you want for me. I am yours. Amen.*

6

Hungry?

"Catch on fire and people will come for miles to watch you burn."

John Wesley

After a few days I learned most of the names of the young people at camp, and I had a pretty good feel for their nuances and quirks. I knew who the loud ones were and who the quiet ones were. Because I had watched the activities, I knew which ones were athletes and who disliked anything strenuous. Without trying to judge I had evaluated which ones came to camp for spiritual reasons and which ones were trying to avoid being touched by God. But as I stood there this evening, I observed something new.

It was the evening meal on the fourth day of camp, and the young people had just come in from a long hike on the mountain behind the campground. They were all dirty, and their hair was out of place. Many of the guys were dripping with sweat, while the young ladies had hints of moisture on their foreheads.

I stood far enough back to hear the conversations of many, watch their postures, and even hear some stomachs growl. They opened the door to the cafeteria, and the line began to move quickly. The guys pushed through the door first almost starting a stampede and coming close to trampling a few of the younger girls who had stationed themselves near the front. Behind the initial push, the line began to take shape. Everyone filled in wherever they fit, a few trying to manipulate their way closer to the doorway while others were satisfied to wait until the line had dwindled down.

Just a few seconds later reports of the menu were beginning to filter through the line: macaroni and cheese, grilled cheese sandwiches, fruit, and of course dessert and the salad bar.

As I eavesdropped on the young people around me, my attention rested on a conversation going on right behind me. Three young men whom I had come to know throughout the course of the week were talking about dinner.

The oldest of the three said he was not hungry. He told his friends that after that much activity he loses his appetite. "So, are you going to pass on dinner?" one asked. "No, because in an hour or two, my appetite will come back and I will be starving."

This young man knew his body. He knew that although he did not have a burning desire to eat right now, there would come a time in the not-too-distant future when he would be hungry if he didn't eat. He was going to eat because he should, not because he felt like it. And in the end he was going to be glad he did.

Because I had to get ready for the service, I got my food and ate it as quickly as I could. Then I headed for my room to shower, change, and pray.

An hour and a half later, I walked into the chapel to find, to my delight, that everyone had showered since our hot excursion. Everyone was looking and smelling good. The sweaty clothes had been replaced with clean ones on the guys, and instead of moisture glistening on the foreheads of the young ladies, they had glittery makeup on. I could smell cologne and perfume in different pockets of the room. As I walked in, I stopped to comment to different people about how good they looked. I asked them how they were doing to get a feel for their mental state before we began the service.

The young man who had not been hungry but had eaten anyway was sitting in a full third row. He said he felt much better after taking a shower. He looked better too, but I wasn't about to tell him that. I went down the row asking how each one was doing. One by one, I got a generic and uneventful "OK" or "good." However, there was one who answered differently. A sixteen-year-old guy sitting toward the end of the row broke the string of positive answers.

"How are you doing?" I asked as I had to the five or six before him.

"I'm hungry," came his response. I told him I hadn't seen him at dinner, and he told me why. "When we got back from our hike, I wanted to get a warm shower. I wasn't hungry at the time, and I thought I would skip dinner."

Now I understood. I offered my sympathy but knew there was nothing I could do to help him fill the void in his stomach. He should have eaten when he could.

No Waiting for Feelings

I realize there are times when we do not have an overwhelming feeling to spend time with God. But if we are to know him, we must spend time with him even when we don't feel like it.

We Christians should live with a depth of intentional desire and hunger that moves us towards Christ. Desire is not about a feeling; it is about a conscious decision to know Christ more intimately. If we don't spend time with him, our spiritual lives will get weak and wither away the same way our physical bodies would break down if we didn't take care of them.

True hunger is a pursuit. You can't wait for the feelings to kick in; you must make it happen. Here are a few ideas for how you can increase your hunger.

Get around Hungry People

One day when we were on the road with our ministry team, we pulled into a restaurant to grab a bite to eat. It was dinnertime and we had been driving all day, but I did not feel hungry. As we were seated and the server took our orders, I chose not to order.

Fifteen minutes passed and I was still not hungry. When the food was delivered to the table, things began to change. I was sitting at a booth with some of my friends who travel with me, and I watched them begin to eat. All three of them began to stuff food in their mouths. Chris had a juicy-looking burger, Reid ordered nachos with extra jalapeños, and Dann was eating some chicken thing.

It wasn't long until the sounds began to indicate that their meals met their expectations. I found myself getting hungry. Watching them eat and seeing the enjoyment on their faces convinced me that I needed something to eat.

Getting the waitress's attention, I ordered a meal. When it came out, I made some of the same noises, and I'm sure I had a smile on my face.

I wasn't going to eat, but when I got around hungry people, I became hungry as well. Spiritually, the same principle applies. If you want to develop desire, get around people who have it. If you want to be a pursuer of Christ, spend time near people who are. As you observe them living their lives and enjoying their spiritual journeys, you will become more hungry. As you see the peace and the joy they exhibit, you will be enticed to try some of what they are having.

Your friends will either dull your spiritual convictions or strengthen them. Choose your companions wisely.

Take Advantage of the Easy Times

Many Christians only go to God in crisis moments. When they are being drawn into sin, they wonder why they don't have more desire for holiness. When they recognize apathy, they ask how they got there.

Don't wait until times get tough to begin to hunger for God's presence and intervention in your life. If you are at a good place in your life spiritually, build from your strength. Take advantage of the peace that you are experiencing right now. Store up for a dry time. Memorize Scripture so that you can take a stand during tough times. Spend time building strength in the Lord now because there will be a time when you will need it. Don't wait until you are in a desperate place. Take advantage of the easy time.

If you are at a good place in your life spiritually, build from your strength.

Avoid Distractions

I am currently writing in a hotel room. I am on the road preparing for a couple of speaking opportunities this week and writing in my spare moments. Knowing that my week was going to be relatively full, I have been trying to knock out a couple of chapters before my hectic schedule kicks in. I got into town about four hours ago and have been working about two of those hours.

I got distracted. I turned on the television and caught a basketball game as it was entering the second quarter. Although I love basketball, I really had no interest in this game. I would have rather been working on this book. Before I knew it, though, the game was over and I hadn't done any work. I ignored my priorities because I got caught up in something less meaningful.

Many people do this spiritually. Their priorities should be their spiritual development, yet they get distracted with other things. Entertainment steals their time and their relationship with the Lord suffers because of it.

If you truly are going to build desire into your life, do your best to avoid distractions. Use good time management and do not let your day slip away without spending time with God.

Some of your distractions may not be sins but still keep you from feeding your spirit. Instead of building strength, these distractions keep you weak and anemic. Look at your life and make note of the things that prove to be unproductive time wasters. Then begin to weed these out of your life.

Ask for Hunger

There is something special for parents about meeting the requests of their kids. Whether my daughter is asking for a drink at bedtime or for help on her homework, the parental side of me jumps to attention. If the request is within reason and if it is something that I am able to provide, there is no question. I will grant it.

God is the perfect Father and he loves his children even more than earthly parents, so we can count on him to do the same. If you want to know God more, ask him. If you want your desire for Christ to increase, request it. In Matthew we read, "If you, then, though you are evil, know how to give good gifts to your children, how much more will your Father in heaven give good gifts to those who ask him!" (Matthew 7:11).

I have begun to recognize that the majority of Christians pray about external things. They pray for friends, family members, their future. Many pray that they will be successful or get good grades. They pray about the big game coming up or the car that they want, but most fail to pray the most intimate prayers.

We need to learn to pray about who we want to be, not just what we want to do. Instead of "Lord, let me play well," we need to spend some time asking God to help us grow spiritually, to deposit strength, character, and hunger into our hearts.

I think it's safe to say young Christian people spend more time praying that God would help them witness better than asking God to make them more Christlike. Witnessing is, of course, very important, but we ought to spend just as much time praying about internal things. If we surrender ourselves in prayer to the Lord in this way, the external things will begin to take care of themselves.

Discipline Yourself

If you were sitting around your house and got hungry, wouldn't you get up and find some food? Many people go through times in their lives when they have no spiritual nourishment, yet they never think to eat. They recognize their thirst but never drink from the living water.

It's vitally important to spend time with Christ, but doing so contradicts everything our society tells us. We spend our energies on the visible aspects of our lives because it seems more immediate. We neglect the unseen parts of our lives even though they are more important and need more attention.

Spiritual strength is not a mystery. It is a matter of discipline. The more time you spend investing in your spiritual life, the stronger you will be. Daily you need to discipline yourself so that God can speak to you, shape you, and mold you.

People who have a strategy for growing in Christ will be strong. People who live by their feelings and leave it to chance will be weak.

Reality Check

- Do you spend most of your time around people who challenge you with their hunger or with people who influence you in the ways of the world? Which people in your life would challenge you to follow Christ?

- What are some strategies that will motivate you to pray even in the good times?

- What things tend to steal your time and distract you from being the committed and growing Christian you want to be?

- How can you reprioritize to make sure you spend your time on what is important?

God, give me a passion for you. I pray that you would become my overwhelming obsession. Begin a hunger in me that will never go out—one that will keep me moving toward you in real and tangible ways. God, I will not wait for the feelings to come before I will draw near to you, but I will discipline myself to spend time with you. Give me some good friends that are hungry for you, so that we can encourage one another in our walk. Help me to avoid the distractions that dominate my time so that I will not waste away the time that I should be using to be with you. You are more precious to me than anything else in this world. May I prove this to you by prioritizing my time appropriately. I ask these things in Jesus' name, because I know that they are your will for me. Amen.

Part 2

prepare for Impact

As you make a habit of spending time with God, your heart will begin to beat the same way his does.

You wouldn't be reading this book unless you wanted to make a difference. You have a dream! You want to work for God and see his kingdom built! You want to leave a legacy of changed lives.

Young people all over are crying out the same thing: "Lord use me!" I believe God loves hearing those words.

As you make a habit of spending time with God, your heart will begin to beat the same way his does. You will have compassion for the lost, and your heart will break for the hurting. In the midst of these feelings, you need to discover how to respond to the world around you. As you begin to look through God's eyes, you will want to speak, serve, and love people with Christ's love. These next chapters are here to help you keep your motives pure as you live out your urges to serve. By serving in Christ, you will have a real and lasting impact on the world.

7

It's Who You Are

"You are more than what you have become."
Mufasa, in *The Lion King*

The scene is epic in my mind: a kingly father declares over his misguided son that he has forgotten who he is and why he exists. The son had been running away from his responsibilities simply because he was having self-esteem issues. He was not even questioning who he was anymore because he had forgotten long ago that he was royalty. Simba was the son of promise and instead of stepping up to fulfill his destiny, he was living in hiding.

No Animation Here

Although this scene took place in an animated movie between two lions in *The Lion King,* I believe there is a spiritual parallel. Young people in every church, community, state, and nation have been hiding from their destiny. In doing so they have forgotten who they are and what God has made them to be. Rather than taking a stand and representing the Lord in this wicked and dark world, they have disappeared.

Some of them will list their excuses and pain. They are living within walls that protect them from conviction, purpose, and making a difference. Others simply don't believe in themselves.

If you are still in hiding, God wants you to know that he is with you. You are his child and you resemble him. Characteristics are in your life that were placed in you the moment you accepted Christ, and they will continue to grow as you walk with him. It is time for you to come out of hiding and put your life on the line for your Lord.

It is time for you to come out of hiding and put your life on the line for your Lord.

If you take a moment, you will sense a change beginning. It is time that God speaks to your heart from above. He wants to remind you of your responsibilities and your duties as a child of God. He will convince you that when you walk with him, you can change your world. If you listen carefully, you will hear the Lord telling you, "You are more than what you have become."

It is time to release the passion that is in your heart. It is time to be courageous for the Lord. God will make you a dominating warrior, a powerful Christian, and an effective ambassador. However, you must come out of hiding.

You Are the Salt of the Earth

The Bible says you are the salt of the earth. "You are the salt of the earth. But if the salt loses its saltiness, how can it be made salty again? It is no longer good for anything, except to be thrown out and trampled by men" (Matthew 5:13). Note that Scripture does not say you have salt; it says you *are* salt. When you surrendered your heart to Christ and entered a relationship with him, a radical change took place in your life. You became salt.

Notice that you were not given a salt shaker that you could ambush people with, rather you were turned into salt. The very essence of who you are is what God will use to influence others around you.

Salt provides unique flavor. You do also. In this world where people are all running around selfishly chasing after things for themselves, you have been created as a selfless substance to be poured out on others to bless them. As Christians we are called to be different, yet too many times we want to be just like the world. You are supposed to influence the world with godly flavor while not letting the world infect you.

Salt exists to be poured out. Salt is useless unless it is used. As a Christian, you can not be satisfied hanging out in church and refusing to go out into the world. God created you to know him, but once you have begun a relationship that is growing with him, your purpose is to overflow into the world.

Many Christians enjoy relationships with other believers so much that they refuse to go out into the world. However, just like salt, your mission will not be completed until you have been poured out into the world.

Salt is a preserving agent. When you live your salty life before Christians without saying a word, you will be reminding them of the commitments they have made to Christ. If there are people around you who are about to make questionable decisions, you may help them remember who they are supposed to be just by being around them.

Weak Christians are looking for someone to lead them. Unless they spend time around salty people who live for Christ, they may not make it. Your impact on their life can be strong.

Salt makes people thirsty. If you are salty, people around you will become thirsty for Christ. They will recognize attributes in your life that point to God's activity, and it will make them want it for themselves.

The problem is that many people in the world have never seen a Christian live a life that is anything close to appetizing to them. They have seen people who walk the fence and do the same things they do, which makes the Christian life unappealing.

You are salt. You have a unique flavor. When you are living passionately for Christ, you will make people thirsty.

Getting Trampled

In Matthew 5:13 Jesus said salt that loses its saltiness is no longer good for anything. It is worthless. Notice he didn't say it becomes something other than salt, he just said it loses attributes that make it salt.

While thinking about this verse, I began to wonder how salt could lose its saltiness. I came up with only one answer. A person who knows Christ loses his or her saltiness by forgetting that he or she is supposed to have a distinct purpose. Christians sometimes try to blend into the world, afraid to show their differences. Such Christians are still salt, but they are not being very salty.

Christians can refuse to be poured out. Opportunities to serve other people selflessly and to be a testimony of what God has done may arise, but Christians who have forgotten they are salty will not take advantage of these opportunities.

By living with weak convictions, Christians lose their ability to be a preserving agent and make people thirsty. They will go to extremes to avoid offending others. In doing this, they are neglecting the capacity they have to influence the world.

As Jesus said, if you lose your saltiness, you are no longer good for anything "except to be thrown out and trampled by men."

I have often wondered why the devil and the world can overpower people who have God in their lives. Many times I have prayed to understand why some young people seemed to get pushed around and taken advantage of by circumstances and people.

I have come to believe that if they refuse to be salty, the world will trample them. If people do not know how to live their lives with purpose and commitment, worldly things will dominate their lives.

If you see in yourself a tendency to get pushed around by your surroundings, maybe it is time for you to evaluate your saltiness. You are salt; live like it!

You Are the Light of the World

The moment that you accepted the Lord, he lit you. We read in Matthew, "You are the light of the world. A city on a hill cannot be hidden. Neither do people light a lamp and put it under a bowl. Instead they put it on its stand, and it gives light to everyone in the house. In the same way let your light shine before men, that they may see your good deeds and praise your Father in heaven" (Matthew 5:14–15). The second that your heart cried out to him, you drew near him. Because he is the light of men (John 1:4), the flame was spread to you.

He did not give you a flashlight or a lighter that you can turn on and off as you please. He did not give you a match that will burn out after a while. He lit you and made you a light to the world. He did not intend you to be hidden but to be visible for the world to see. You are to shine in the darkness and be an ambassador of light.

Again, you are different. If you are living for Christ, you are going to stand out. People are going to notice you and the life that you lead. They will recognize the external things that are different (i.e., the lifestyle that you live will be different from that of other people your age), but they will also recognize what God is doing deep inside you. They will see your peace in the midst of difficulties, your love in the face of adversity. People will realize that you have an ability to trust God rather than your emotions. As people see these things, they will be drawn to them. They will want them.

For the most part he wants you to do things that people will observe before you start talking.

Silent Movers

In making you the salt of the earth and the light of the world, God wants you to be seen before you are heard. He did not make you the "foghorn of the world" so that people would hear you coming from miles away before seeing the fruit of your life. For the most part he wants you to do things that people will observe before you start talking.

If you live a salty life and if you let your light shine, your witness will be effective. You won't have to convince people of your claims; you will spend most of your time answering questions about what is different about you.

Godly young people can be silent movers, quiet change agents.

Speak Up If You Have the Opportunity

I am not saying you should not look for opportunities to speak truth to people; I am simply saying usually the people that you are sharing with, depending on their relationship with you, should see it before they hear it.

Actually, I encourage you to pray for and look for opportunities to say something about what you know to be true about God. However, be sensitive to the Spirit of God as you are looking to share about him.

I have seen many people who were closed to the gospel become open because someone showed them love or served them selflessly. When Christians concentrate on expressing the gospel in actions, they set the stage for words to be effective.

It Is Who You Are

Face the facts and stop running from the truth. The moment you surrendered your heart to Christ, you became different. He changed who you are. You are light, you are salt. You are a change agent and a history maker. You can live a radical existence. It is possible for you to be a contagious Christian.

Up until this point, you may not have been living up to it, but you are what God needs. He created you and crafted you specifically for this day and age. It is time that you live up to who you are. There is greatness in you!

Reality Check

- Have you ever heard God tell you that "you are more than what you have become"? Are there certain ways that you tend to hide from who he has made you to be?

- What do you see when you look in the mirror? A victor or a victim? Do you see greatness? Do you see the Father's reflection?

- What does "the salt of the earth mean to you"?

- Have you ever found yourself hiding your light? When do you tend to do it most?

- In what areas can people see Christ in your life? Which areas do you need to work on?

God, I pray *that you would teach me to see myself the way that you see me. When I look in the mirror, Lord, allow me to see myself as a child of yours who has the ability to impact and influence my world. You have made me light and you have made me salt. God, forgive me for the times when I have hidden that light or forgotten who I was. I want to be everything that you have called me to be. I will speak when you tell me to, and do all that I can to show your light to all those around me. Continue to work in me so that I can become who you desire me to be. I love you. Amen.*

8

The Gospel's Motivation: Love

"I want a life spent in putting other people right."
William Booth

Adam was a young man determined to be a preacher. He had been introduced to Jesus Christ at the age of sixteen, and at that time he fell in love with the idea of being on stage. When special speakers and traveling ministers would come through our church, Adam was intrigued by their stories of supernatural boldness that resulted in people accepting Christ. With every speaker and with every story, the fire would burn brighter in his heart to have his own stories to tell.

When Adam had been walking with the Lord for just a short time, he began to tell me about all the people he was telling about the Lord. Not having picked up on his motivation for telling me this, I applauded him. After all, not many young people are willing to step out and share about Christ at all.

However, it was not long before I began to notice a few trends that disturbed me. Whenever the microphone was available for testimonies, Adam was up there sharing about someone whom he had told about Christ. Sometimes three times a month, Adam talked about meeting someone on the street and turning the conversation to Christ. The things that began to worry me were:

- He seemed to enjoy the spotlight. By sharing his stories, he gained exposure, and the people around him began to recognize him as a real "go-getter." On more than one occasion, I heard people compliment his heroic acts of witnessing, and he seemed to soak in the attention.
- He never talked about anyone making a decision for Christ, only about him telling them they needed to. Although it is not our job to make people accept Christ, if shared the correct way, I think the message will be appealing. I couldn't quite put my finger on it, but something about his stories seemed lopsided.
- I discovered his method was not based in love. While visiting a school one day, I met a girl who knew Adam. As I began to talk with her, I discovered quickly she was not at all interested in the gospel. Using questions, I discovered that a few young people had assaulted her with their evangelism. Adam was one of the main perpetrators.

When I discovered these things, I knew that something needed to be done. I began a process of talking with Adam about his motivation for sharing Christ and also about his method.

The only reason to share the Lord is out of love. If you love the Father and want his message broadcast, you witness. If you love the people around you, you want the best for them. Naturally, the gospel message is the most captivating of all time, and the benefits stand alone. About love Jesus said, "Love the Lord your God with all your heart and with all your soul and with all your mind. This is the first and greatest commandment. And the second is like it: Love your neighbor as yourself" (Matthew 22:37–39). Unless Adam learned how to operate in love, he would do more harm than good.

Love is the proper motive and it is the perfect method. People must sense that you love them before they will receive your methods.

God Is Making You More Loving

Without God's help, you wouldn't have the ability to love others. However, the moment that you began your journey with God, he changed some things in your heart. When you experienced love from God, you were given the ability to love others (1 John 4:19).

God opened up your heart and poured his love into it (Romans 5:5)—not just a little, but an overwhelming amount. Your heart is being saturated by his love.

The result of God's work in your life is the fruit of his spirit. The more you walk with the Lord in a surrendered state, the more your life will be producing the fruit of the spirit (Galatians 5:22–23). One of the fruits recorded is love.

God redefined love. As humans, we have a limited capacity to love. We find it easier to love those who treat us well, but God's kind of love is perfect (1 Corinthians 13), even for those who have done wrong. As we experience this kind of unconditional love, we begin to recognize it in its purest form. Because we have received it, we are able to give it away as well.

Love As the Foundation

Love is to be the very foundation of our lives. Our Christianity is based on love. Because God loved us even though we were not worthy, he sent his only son. Jesus died on the cross out of love for you and me. In return, we are to love others. The love that we receive from God should make us willing to love those around us.

Love Is a Command

God did not request that we love others, he commanded it. He did not leave us any other option. Out of obedience to him, we must learn to love. He did not leave us room for compromise or excuse. We cannot tell God, "I'm sure you wouldn't want me to love him because he has been really mean to me."

When God commanded you to love people, he knew ahead of time that people would be mean to you. He knew the things they would say about you, the pain they would cause you, and the way they would take advantage of you. He knew all of these things, but he still commanded that you love them. In his command, there is no room for compromise. If you fail to love someone, you are walking in disobedience to God.

How Do I Learn to Love?

If you are like me, then love is not your first thought. Your human nature has a tendency to be bitter and vengeful instead of loving and accepting. If someone dislikes you,

you dislike him or her. If someone has wronged you, you feel like you have a right to withhold love from him or her. Did a person make you feel stupid or say things about you behind your back? Then you should have the right to get even, shouldn't you?

The biblical answer is no. There is never a reason to be anything other than loving to everyone that you meet. So, if your nature is unloving, but your calling is to love, how do you make the transition? Here are a couple of ideas for you.

God did not request that we love others, he commanded it.

Spend Time with God

In 1 John 4:8 and 1 John 4:16, the Bible says God is love. If you spend time with him, you will become what he is. I have seen evidence of this principle in my own life. There have been many times when I have walked with a minimal amount of love. Certain people grated against me and made me angry. It's hard to love when you are angry, so I was anything but kind to them. I hurt some of them badly.

When evaluating my life, I noticed a trend. The more time I was spending with God, the fewer people I was hurting. When I was having regular times alone with the Lord, I wasn't acting out in bitterness or anger. However, when I was "too busy" for God, I was finding time to wound people I should have been encouraging.

As you take time to saturate your heart in the Word of God, you are giving an invitation to God to prune your attitudes and shape your temperament.

If you are trying to improve in the area of loving people, start here. Make sure that you are spending time with the Lord.

Be Intentional about Loving Others

Love is not a feeling, it is a choice. Sure, there are times when I feel a special appreciation or fondness for someone, but that is rare. More often than not, loving people is something I choose to do.

Sometimes love is a matter of getting past irritated feelings, while other times it is simply a matter of overruling apathetic tendencies. There are times when I don't want to love and other times when I forget that I am supposed to.

The Bible tells us we are supposed to spend time thinking about how we can help others love better: "And let us consider how we may spur one another on toward love and good deeds" (Hebrews 10:24). Instead of sitting on our beds at night plotting revenge against someone who embarrassed us, we should take time to figure out how to encourage them. Give careful thought to how you can show your love for people.

Ellen was great at this. She was a youth leader who worked with me for about two years. Although a few things got under her skin, she never showed it to the kids. Instead, she loved intentionally every chance she got. Rather than giving a random hug that might not be recognized as sincere, she would send notes of encouragement. On occasion she would buy gifts to express her deep feelings and commitment to the young people. Other times she would bless them with a random phone call.

Misty was a young lady I met only once, but I quickly saw she was well liked, and I soon found out why. In the lunch line at this camp where I was speaking, she would come in with notes for new students she had just met. People's faces would glow as they read her encouraging words. I am sure my face shone with surprise, yet joy, as I read the one she gave me. Every day at this camp, Misty, a very normal and popular girl, took some of her free time to be intentional about encouraging others.

Be intentional about loving others. If you wait until you feel like loving people, you may be waiting a long time. However, if you take specific calculated actions to show others that you love them and value them, you will be obeying God's command to love.

Serve Others

I hate to admit it to the public, but parts of me are shallow and immature. Sometimes this becomes very visible in my relationships. Over the years I have been around many people that just irritated me. It was not their fault, it was mine. They were being themselves, but because I was inconvenienced, I put walls up to keep them out.

I have been praying that God would strip me of these tendencies, and I have begun to notice a difference. In the last several months I have made it a priority to take steps to serve people who bug me, and 100 percent of the time it has worked. The moment that I begin to serve someone, no matter how much they exasperated me, my attitude about them changed. The first act of doing something nice for them stripped me of my ill feelings. Let me give you an example.

Last summer I was speaking at a camp. One girl there was really getting on my nerves. She was whiny and always begging for attention. Because I was the speaker, she targeted me as someone from whom she especially needed attention.

For the first three meals of the camp, this girl sat next to me and monopolized the conversation so that I couldn't meet any of the other young people. After the meal she followed me around and hovered over me. After twenty-four hours of this, I was getting irritated. Even the sound of her voice was beginning to grate on me. When she would tell a story, I didn't want to listen, and when I did catch part of one of her unbelievable tales, I felt like I needed to point out her exaggerations and lies. I was not sure if I was going to make it through the week without wounding her in a moment of rage.

True servanthood is contagious.

Then it happened. Without thinking, I served her. It was the fourth meal and she was sitting next to me. After sitting for three minutes, she let out this pathetic little whine about forgetting to get a beverage. I quickly jumped up to get it for her.

When she saw me move, she grabbed my arm and told me she didn't want me to get it for her, but I insisted. The craziest thing happened. The moment I returned with her soft drink, my attitude was different. Instead of seeing her as an obnoxious, selfish, needy little girl, I recognized her as someone who needed love.

I had no idea that I was going to be influenced that much by a quick thirty-second errand for a fifteen-year-old girl, but I was. That moment I decided to serve all of the young people and the counselors whenever I could. I began at that meal to make several trips to the dishwasher with people's trays. People would try and stop me, but I didn't want to stop. I was not doing it because I had to, nor was I doing it with a bad attitude, I wanted to serve them. And by serving them physically, it helped me better serve them emotionally and spiritually.

Before I end the story, I want to tell you about one weird thing that happened later that week, and I have seen it happen several times since. Others began to carry trays also. Instead of me being the only one to help clean off tables, a few others began to serve their leaders and peers the same way. It also spilled into other areas of the camp. True servanthood is contagious. If you are having problems loving someone, try serving them. I bet your attitude will change.

Concentrate on the Tough Ones

The Bible makes it clear that you are to love all people. That does not give you permission to love the 90 percent you like. You must love everyone. And because some people are easy to love, I recommend spending more energy on those who are difficult to love.

Certain people have made themselves difficult to love. Maybe they did something annoying or have a negative attitude. Maybe they don't return your love. Whatever the reason, you may feel justified in refusing to love them. But you are not. I cannot find any excuse that God will accept for a failure to love anyone.

I have had people tell me that I am a terrible youth pastor and a horrific preacher. I had one young man tell me after a service that he thought I was a jerk. Another teenager told me he didn't respect me. I have had all the cuss words ever used aimed at me both behind my back and directly to my face. People have tried to discredit me and they have lied about me, but I am still commanded by God to love them.

Although every one of those people hurt me, I found no right to avoid loving them (and I looked). I had to come to grips with the fact that their behavior did not govern whether or not I should love them, God's Word did. Whether or not they treated me well didn't matter, I had to love them.

Back to Adam

At the beginning of this chapter I introduced you to Adam, who was sharing the gospel with the wrong motivation. After I realized how Adam was approaching people, I began spending time with him. Over the course of a couple months he began to understand that his motivation for serving others was supposed to be love. When he began to understand this, I taught him how to love people into the kingdom instead of preaching at them.

I saw a softening take place in Adam's life. His increased time with God and his love for people were beginning to pay off. He was reaching out more and being better received by other people in the youth group. On occasion I even saw him praying with a younger attendee on the corner of our stage after a service. One night after youth group I saw him leaving with one of the young people whom some considered an outcast. Adam was taking him out for dessert and to spend time with him.

God was doing something in Adam's heart. Adam wasn't always looking for the spotlight. Instead of lifting himself up, he seemed to be making a conscious effort to point out the positive things in other people.

Then it happened. On a Tuesday afternoon Adam came bounding into my office. There was joy in his eyes, and he was visibly excited. His heart was racing so much he couldn't contain himself. He told me he led someone to Christ. The person's name was Clayton who was a loner in school. Everyone avoided him because he was weird.

About three weeks earlier Adam noticed Clayton sitting all by himself in the lunch room. Adam joined him. Not because he wanted to, but because he wanted Clayton to know that he wasn't alone and that someone cared. Adam told me that for the first two weeks, he did not share Jesus with his new friend but concentrated on communicating acceptance.

However, on Monday, Clayton opened up about some things going on in his home. He trusted Adam with this information because he knew Adam cared. Adam listened and began to share how Jesus wanted to help him deal with the stress of the situation. From there, the conversation led to knowing Jesus as a friend and how Adam had surrendered his heart to him. Right there at the lunch table, Adam prayed with Clayton to accept Christ.

As Adam bounced around my office, he told me that it was the first time he had ever led someone to Christ. He realized that when he openly showed Clayton that he cared about him, his message was received.

We prayed together that day. Adam has since led many people to Christ and was a positive influence in our youth ministry until the day he graduated. Now he is in college, loving people and telling them about Jesus. When his motive became love and his method changed, he became effective for the Lord. If you want to be effective at making Christ known, develop your ability to love.

Reality Check

- Do you believe you are walking in love toward the people with whom you'd like to share Christ, or on occasion do you have a selfish and possibly prideful agenda?

- How can you improve your ability to love others? Have you been connecting with God when you are alone and asking him to help you love others?

- How did you come to Christ?

- ✸ What can you do today or tomorrow to show someone that you care?

Father, you are the one *who loves perfectly. Teach me. Show me how to love the people that grate on me and care about those that I would rather ignore. God, make me one of those people that is continually being used to reach those that the world considers to be unlovely. As I go out of my way to show them that they are valuable, may they understand the message of your love. Give me creative ideas, increase my patience, and teach me to serve others. Lord, you were the perfect example of these things, may I represent you in love. May they see you in my actions, attitudes, and service. All that I do, I do for you. Amen.*

9

Lessons Learned from an Older Sibling

"God can do more through one man who is 100% dedicated to him than through 100 men who are only 90% dedicated."
DAWSON TROTMAN

I had the distinct pleasure of working with my brother, Byron, a couple of times when we were growing up, and whenever I did, I learned a lot from him. I respect him a great deal for working harder than anyone else and effectively handling any responsibilities that were given to him.

When we were both teenagers, we worked at a greasy hamburger stand in Spokane, Washington. This was my first real job, and it was hard work that taught me a lot. I learned how to deal with stress. (When I first started working there, I woke up with nightmares three or four nights in a row.) I learned how to put all of my heart into tasks that were not glamorous. (Certain responsibilities were either disgusting in nature or incredibly monotonous.) Also, I learned how to take ownership of a job I didn't like.

Most of these things I learned from Byron. Although there were moments when I did not enjoy working with my brother, many times I was glad to have him around. When we would get a rush of customers, he was the man.

Because this place sits right on the freeway and serves good but cheap food, there were times when we got swamped. People came out of nowhere (sometimes by the busload) to order our burgers and fries. When we got hit hard, Byron saved us.

Whenever a surge began, they called Byron off break. They left other people on break, because they didn't help all that much when they were working, but not my brother. He came up front, put his hat back on, and began to work. He was a blur. He started behind the grill, helping lay out the eighty burger patties that filled the grill. When all the hamburger was down, he took buns out of the toaster and began to help put condiments on the buns. When he got a spare minute, he ran over to the fry area to sack, cook, or put together the other things served from that area. If people were falling behind on taking orders, he stepped up to the front counter and called out, "Can I help someone down here."

He was everywhere. Sometimes these rushes would last for an hour, and Byron made sure that we all kept up with our responsibilities. He never thought certain jobs were beneath him; he was concentrating on making sure that the entire restaurant was doing what it was supposed to do. He was always working for and improving the reputation of the establishment.

When the managers looked at the calendar, if there was a day when they were going to be more busy than normal, guess who was scheduled first? I am convinced he was the best they had to offer. They needed him. Tough job? Byron will do it. Need something done quickly? Where is Byron? Who do you trust to close? Byron!

I was an employee, but Byron was a special employee. I did my job well, but Byron did his job exceptionally, and he made everybody else better. Several years ago I learned what it meant to be a great employee and a good worker by watching my brother.

The Great Commission

As Christians, we have been given a job to do. We are to preach the gospel and make disciples wherever we go. Jesus said, "Go into all the world and preach the good news to all creation" (Mark 16:15). We are to take the truth of Christ and convince people that they need to surrender to him. We can either take this job seriously and be effective, or we can be half-hearted in our attempts.

I decided a long time ago that I wanted to be a great employee of the kingdom of God. There is a rush coming, a revival that is going to hit, and I don't want to be stuck taking a break. I want to do anything and everything I can to take part in the harvest.

By looking at Byron's attitude when he was a teenager cooking and serving burgers, I believe we can glean things that will help us be effective.

A Sense of Urgency

Whenever Byron worked there was urgency. He took his responsibilities very seriously and it could be seen in his actions, heard in his words, and felt when you were around him.

If he was that urgent about serving burgers, don't you think Christians should be even more earnest about spreading the gospel and making disciples? If Byron was somewhat slow in performing his duties, someone might have to wait an extra couple of minutes before they could feed themselves. If we as Christians are slow, someone's life and eternal destination may be affected.

We should live with an urgency that forces us to pray hard and long. This same urgency will push us out of our comfort zones and encourage us to open our mouths. It will not let us be content when people in our presence are in desperate need of the answers we have been given.

If we live without urgency, we will waste our time, keep our mouths shut, and stay to ourselves. We must understand that our task is vitally important. It must drive us. We cannot be content when we know there are people who need the Lord. We must not be complacent, but we must live with an aggressive approach to sharing the gospel.

Many different analogies emphasize how seriously we should take our responsibility of sharing the gospel. People are sick and we have the medicine to cure them. Without it, they have no hope of living. If they inject the medicine, they will live. A bunch of people are on a plane that is destined to crash. You have been given parachutes to distribute to other passengers. The more parachutes you distribute, the more lives will be saved.

All the analogies I've heard are great because they convey the urgency of our situation and the responsibility of those who know the truth. You must rush to their aid because you have the medicine that will cure their disease. You need to move quickly to give away as many parachutes as possible.

We must live with the seriousness of an emergency situation. All of the people who have not surrendered their hearts to Christ are in critical condition. You have the cure. It is time for you to come off break and spread the good news.

He Was Always Alert

When Byron would come to work, he was always alert. He always noticed when someone was starting to fall behind. Because he was always looking, he was able to rush to the aid of those who were struggling.

God wants us to be alert. When we walk around our community, into our schools and churches, we need to pray for discernment. We always should be looking for warning signs in the faces of the individuals we talk with. We should be ready to answer their questions, reduce their pain, and drive off their fear.

Wherever you walk, you can let God speak to you about the condition of the world and the people in it. He will teach you how to pray, what to say to people, how and when to act. By alertly looking around you, you will increase your effectiveness at sharing the gospel. You will know when to speak and when not to. You will see opportunities to speak hope and life into people's day.

Some Christians take the "bull in a china shop" approach to spreading the gospel. Instead of being led by the Spirit of God, they start preaching whenever and to whomever they want. By being alert, you will be more effective and see more fruit as you work with the Lord to share your faith with those around you.

He Was Quick to the Task

Many times I saw Byron leave what he was doing to help someone else. He didn't hide behind his job description and rationalize his way to the least amount of work he could do; he did whatever needed to be done. He served selflessly with no regard to being recognized by the management. Many people will serve if they will get noticed, but as a Christian you should serve so God will be noticed.

If Byron saw a need, he was quick to meet it. He didn't wait to be asked. Many times he did not ask the manager permission to go help somebody out, he just adjusted to meet the need. Although this may sound rebellious, it was not. Other people might have seen the need, but because they did not want to create more work for themselves, they would not help out. My brother was different.

If you are praying for God to use you, get ready to serve in some abnormal ways.

If you are praying for God to use you, get ready to serve in some abnormal ways. You may think he is preparing you for some great ministry that will bring you notoriety in the future, but you will get there only if you are willing to meet the needs that are before you right now.

You may be called to preach someday, but what about sharing with the unpopular lonely kid at school? What about the problem that your church is having finding nursery workers? Maybe God is waiting to see if you will be faithful with little things before he entrusts you with much.

What about the work day that the church has coming up? I know it is on Saturday and you wanted to sleep in, but great employees of the kingdom meet needs. No matter how small, no matter what day of the week, people who serve God serve others as well.

Be quick to the task, don't wait for someone to ask you to help, and don't take months praying about whether God wants you to serve in this way. If you become aware of a need and you have the ability to meet it, jump in and make it happen.

He Had a Great Attitude about Work

When Byron walked through the door to work, he left his problems outside. He always had a great attitude. When you are serving Christ, which you should be doing all the time if you're a Christian, you need to have a great attitude. You can't complain or whine about people or projects God has given you. Don't argue with God about the part you play in the scheme of things; be grateful he has chosen you for his team.

I know several Christians who have terrible attitudes. They don't want to serve in church. They don't want to share their faith, which is good because these people turn non-Christians off anyway, and they talk God out of using them.

I think God gets tired of hearing all the excuses these people have. Because in the past they have not served with sincere desire, they have not done a good job. Therefore, because of their excuses, lack of motivation, terrible work ethic, and the poor job they have done in the past, I believe God stops calling them to serve. I think he gets so fed up with whiners and complainers that he overlooks them in search of someone who has a good attitude and wants to be used.

He Was a Good Teacher along the Way

It didn't matter how busy the rush was, Byron was always teaching. If the fry guy was falling behind, Byron was there to help him catch up. But he was showing him why he fell behind. If the people taking the orders at the window were losing the battle, he would help them out and teach them tricks to make them better at their jobs.

When you are growing with God, you have a responsibility not only to those who don't know Christ, but also to those who are Christians living where you have been.

Instead of doing all of the serving, praying, witnessing, and so on, you should be teaching others along the way.

Your youth group is likely to include people who need the encouragement and instruction that you can offer them. Some of them need to know how to share their faith; others need to be encouraged to have daily times with God. As a peer, you might be just the one to teach them these things.

Every day you need to look for people to encourage. Encourage them in their walk with Christ, challenge them out of their comfort zones, and take them into places where they have to trust God. Great employees of the kingdom don't do all the work, but they invest in others so more work gets done.

For Every Byron There's a Tim

Byron was a great employee, but several people were the exact opposite of Byron. There were people like Tim, who was intentionally slow at his work. He cut every corner he could if it saved him work. He had a terrible attitude and he was a huge distraction to those he was working with. Although they never fired him, I believe they should have.

Tim was the type of guy who never moved fast. Everyone else would be handling at least four customers at once; he was content with one. During a rush, everyone moved quickly and with purpose but not Tim. He would spend extra time filling up his drink, because he wouldn't have to take extra orders that way.

If Tim was alert, he didn't want anyone to know. He purposely failed to notice things that needed to get done so that he wouldn't have to do more work. If he would run out of cups, he wouldn't stock them; he would wait until someone else did it. Instead of making others better, his laziness spread to those around him.

I got frustrated with him on several occasions. I wanted him to do his job. He had been hired to help sell and serve burgers. He was a poor representation of the establishment and terrible at customer service.

For every person who approaches the great commission like Byron approached his job, many approach it like Tim. The majority of Christians have no urgency when it comes to spreading the good news. They don't see the vast needs that surround them and when they do recognize them, they don't rush to meet them. Quite a few Christians have bad attitudes about sharing the gospel and letting their faith be seen. And although I hate to admit this, many Christians hinder others from living aggressively and preaching boldly.

If God were to send you a spiritual report card that told you how you approached spreading the most exciting message ever known, would you be a Byron or a Tim? Are you a great employee of the kingdom of God, a bad employee, or just average?

God needs some great people to rise up from your generation. Don't you want him to call you off break when revival hits?

Reality Check

- Is there urgency in your approach to sharing and demonstrating your faith?

- When you see a need, are you quick to meet it or do you sometimes avoid it simply because it is an inconvenience to you?

- Do you have a good attitude about serving people and God? How is your attitude in regard to sharing your faith? Do you see it as a duty or a privilege? If your attitude needs changing, what can you do today that will help?

- Which people do you think God might want you to encourage?

- If you are going to be a great employee in the kingdom of God, which lesson that I learned from Byron do you need to work on most?

Lord, I want to be *a good employee for your kingdom. I want to be quick to the task and urgent in my approach. God, give me discernment to see the needs that are before me and the wisdom to know how to let you meet them. Help me to bring your hope to everyone I meet. I pray that you find me trustworthy. Make me more like you, Jesus. Amen.*

10

practical Tips for Sharing your faith

"O, God, Give me souls or I will die."
John Hyde

Four or five youth workers and I were attending a training convention to improve our skills in youth ministry. As an exercise, we were sent out to start up a conversation with teenagers. We had to look for opportunities to turn our conversation to spiritual things and see where it led.

After a quick dinner we prayed in the van, then drove to a movie theater to see if teenagers were hanging around outside on this Friday night. Sure enough there were several. We stepped out of the van into the parking lot not knowing what the results would be. We knew only one thing; we were going to tell some teenagers about Jesus.

Because I had done this before, I was not intimidated. However, some of the other youth workers were. They chose to let me begin the conversation (I love talking to strangers). Walking up to a circle of six people who looked to be about fifteen years old, I invaded their conversation. "What are your names?" You could tell by the looks on their faces that they were slightly confused. "Why is this old guy talking to us?" But the question was direct, so they responded by telling us their names. Answering our additional questions, they shared their ages and the schools they attended.

I introduced my friends and told them we were youth workers. I admitted to them that while we worked with teenagers on a weekly basis, sometimes in the confines of our churches we weren't able to get a good idea of what the public schools are like. I asked them if they could answer a few questions for us.

Understanding that we were interested in them, they were more than happy to give us a bit of their time. Their parents had dropped them off early for the movie, and they were just killing time anyway. Two of the girls were laughing uncomfortably and whispering, but the others were very willing to talk with us.

"Do you go to church?" Two did on a weekly basis, two did on occasion, and two didn't. Perfect. They would provide a wide range of answers to the questions I would ask them. I hoped to encourage the church attendees to think about their convictions and to introduce the others to Jesus who is the reason for church attendance.

By simply finding out about their families ("Do you live with both parents, stepparents, or one?"), their habits ("Do you 'party'?"), their interests ("What are the most important things in your lives?"), and their dreams ("Where do you think you will be in ten years and what kind of a person do you want to be?"), I earned their trust. You can easily earn someone's trust by listening attentively. From that point on, I gave them a simple way that Jesus could relate to their lives.

They listened closely and began to ask their own questions. Within fifteen minutes I had explained the gospel. I did not talk about church or religion, but about Jesus. They paid close attention as I described how Jesus had died on the cross with their lives in the balance. Very quickly I explained how they needed to surrender their lives to his will and walk in relationship with him.

In the few minutes we had, I did not have enough time to describe in detail how his plan for their lives was better than the things that they had planned for themselves, but I communicated his unconditional love for them.

As show time drew closer, I asked them how they felt about Jesus and the relationship that I had described. Three said they needed to surrender their lives to Jesus and begin to build a relationship with him. Two said they were already Christians but realized they needed to live by their convictions and walk more closely with him. The other one said he was not interested in Jesus at this point.

In the parking lot we held hands and prayed for the five people who wanted to walk in a relationship with the Lord. As we left, we encouraged the young ladies who went to a youth group to begin to take their friends and to tell their youth leader about the renewed commitments they had made. As we climbed into the van, we asked what had surprised us. We mentioned several things:

- Most were surprised that the young people were willing to talk with us at all, let alone that they seemed to enjoy it.

- We were caught off guard by how honest they were when they realized we were truly interested in their lives. One woman commented that she was shocked when they freely answered my question about which drugs they had tried.
- We were surprised by how moral they seemed. Although they did things that we disagreed with, they didn't do them out of rebellion. They made poor choices because society had convinced them there were no absolutes.
- Finally, our group was amazed at how open to the gospel these young people were. Five of the six wanted to walk with Jesus.

That night God got his wish with those five young people.

Young People Are Advancing the Kingdom

Some may say youth leaders are supposed to share their faith and be effective, but I have known many young people who have led several to the Lord. Sometimes they introduce their friends to the Lord, and other times they do so with people they meet out in public.

Stories are always coming to me:

- A young lady led several members of her basketball team to the Lord.
- A lifeguard led three friends to Christ by the pool after work.
- Two friends started a conversation with three adolescents at a water park and ended up praying with them to surrender their hearts to Jesus.

In these coming years some students are going to make some noise in the area of evangelism. Few will be the traditional evangelists who hold a microphone and sport a navy blazer and an expensive tie. However, there will be many who share their faith often and promote God's message.

Students all over the world will be aggressive with the gospel, and people will respond to them. These people will be urgent in their approach and effective in their style. If you are waiting for the Lord to demand you to be a part of this evangelistic army, he will not. You must enlist. If your desire is to join what God is going to do, you can be one of the effective ones. Here are some practical tips to help you in your approach to evangelism.

Always Keep Your Eyes Open for Opportunities

You never know when an opportunity to talk about Christ will present itself, so be looking. When having conversations with friends, waitresses, or with people in passing, you might find the perfect opportunity.

You never know when an opportunity to talk about Christ will present itself, so be looking.

If you see people who are having a difficult time, introduce them to the God who will help. Do you know someone who has been taken advantage of by a friend? Tell him or her about the one who will be a perfect friend. Do you know someone who's been hurt? Tell him or her about the one who was wounded for them.

Wherever you look, people need what Christ offers. If you listen well and watch closely, with God's help you will begin to see how much they need the Lord's touch. After you see it, you must be faithful to say what needs to be said.

Be Confident in What You Are Presenting

Confidence is visible. If you believe in what you are saying, you can boldly stand before anyone and tell them the truth. Some people will aggressively confront opinions that differ from theirs in many areas. They will confidently talk about their hobbies, politics, or sports. Many times they will debate things they believe in. However, the same people often become weak and have no passion when it comes to faith.

If you are going to share your faith, you better believe in it. You better know that you are offering people the greatest thing available.

A few years ago I was in the middle of a fundraising project. Our ministry was raising money for a specific program that would allow us to reach several thousand young people. One day I got a check in the mail accompanied by a letter. The person who wrote was a friend from Florida who loved me enough to tell me the truth. He explained that my fundraising letter was too apologetic, and he told me that if I did not believe my cause was the most important cause in the world, I should not be asking people for help.

He was right. By not wanting to offend people, I had forgotten that I was asking them to support something that I believe is of utmost importance. I lacked visible confidence, and it was obvious to everyone around. Since that time I have regularly checked my confidence level. I do not want to fall into a rut and act out of a routine. I want to operate out of conviction and passion.

When sharing your faith, I encourage you to do the same thing. Do you believe the message you are about to present? Are you really convinced that everyone needs Jesus and will be desperately sorry one day if they don't surrender to him? If you believe it, act like it. If you don't believe it, stop talking.

Ask Good Questions

Whether I'm talking to people in line at the Epcot Center, a waitress in a restaurant, or a teenager at a camp, I always ask questions. People love to talk about themselves. You begin to win their trust by listening. And if you ask the right questions, you can get a feel for where they are, in their families, socially, and spiritually.

Some general questions always precede deeper questions. "What is your name?" "Where are you from?" "What school do you go to?" These things get you in the door. Then you begin to dig a little bit.

Sometimes people will give you a direction to take with your next question as you listen to the answer of the previous one. "Where are you from?" might inform you that this person just moved to the area with her mom after her parents' recent divorce. From there an "Oh, bummer. Was the divorce hard on you?" will get you headed in a direction that might give you insight into their spiritual needs.

If you are actively looking for opportunities to share your faith, you would be wise to save your words and listen until you have a specific direction that you want to go. Questions will help you do this.

Do Not Be Ashamed of What You Stand For

If you are talking with someone and they realize that you are embarrassed or not totally convinced of what you are saying, they will not take you seriously. When I was in high school, I used to try to share my faith with people at work. To me that meant sharing Jesus with people who didn't know him as well as encouraging weaker Christians to be stronger.

One of the Christians who had problems living for the Lord was Kelly. She had grown up in a good home but had walked away from God. When she was sixteen, she had recommitted her life to the Lord, but there were many things pulling her away. In prayer one day, I felt like God wanted me to encourage her. I asked the Lord how and he gave me a creative way.

One afternoon I brought a few 3 x 5 cards with Bible verses on them to work. They were stuck in my back pocket and whenever I would get a spare moment I would pull them out and work on committing them to memory. Although I did not ask Kelly if she wanted to participate, I knew she would. When she saw me memorizing the verses, she began to do the same. When I was done with a verse, she would take it and commit it to memory.

For five or six days we did this. In an eight-hour shift, we could memorize three to five verses. Utilizing idle moments, we were storing up God's Word in our hearts.

Less than a week into this, one of Kelly's friends saw us in the break room with our cards. After Kelly's break was over, she asked me what we were doing with those cards. I told her. That's when Kelly got upset. She was embarrassed. When I went back up to the front, she came up to me and said, "Why did you tell her what we were doing?"

I told Kelly I didn't want to be ashamed about my faith and that is why I was willing to tell a non-Christian about my relationship with Christ. When I found the boldness to tell others about my relationship with the Lord, it strengthened my faith even more. As I was explaining this to Kelly, I saw the light go on. I literally saw her face change as she began to understand that she was supposed to be proud of the relationship she had with Christ.

"Do you think I should tell Jenny what we are doing?" Jenny was a girl who had taken Kelly out to parties and gotten her into trouble in the past. Up to this point, Kelly had not wanted her to know that she was trying to live for the Lord. I told her she should do whatever she believed the Lord wanted her to do.

Kelly turned around quickly, went up to Jenny, and said, "Do you know what I just did? I just memorized a verse in the Bible. 'I am not ashamed of the gospel, for it is the power of God for the salvation of everyone who believes.'" It was an instant change. Kelly realized she had something that everyone needed, and she wasn't going to hide it anymore. From that moment on people began to take her faith seriously because they saw the strong conviction she had.

If you are going to share your faith effectively, you shouldn't be ashamed. Be proud.

If You Are Talking to a Group, Focus on One

It is very difficult to talk to a group about something that is so personal. The more spread out your attention is, the harder it will be. One way to limit distractions is to focus on one person. This does not mean you should ignore the others, just that you should concentrate your attention on only one person.

In the first several minutes of a conversation, you will be able to determine which person in the group is most interested, most open, and most willing to get beyond shallow conversation. Look directly at this person and listen intently to him or her.

When I am sharing with a small group of people, I tend to have an in-depth conversation with one person while not ignoring everyone else. Everyone else is listening, and occasionally I will include the others. However, for the most part I aim my attention and conversation at my focal point as I share the gospel.

Don't Focus on Small Things, Stay Directed at the Main Thing

Matt ran into the youth room one Wednesday night. As soon as I finished preparing for the service, I called him over to let him say what he had been wanting to tell me since the minute he walked into the room.

"I shared the gospel with Jim today," he said excitedly.

"That's great," I told him. "Tell me about it."

"I was in the lunch room today and I heard Jim and some guys talking about the party that they were going to this weekend. Pretty soon I had heard enough. I walked over to their table and told them they shouldn't party. I told them it wasn't good for them. Then I told them I was a Christian, had never drunk any alcohol, and I never would."

That's where Matt stopped. That was the extent of his story. He rebuked Jim and his friend for their actions and thought that was sharing the gospel.

I very lovingly took some time and taught Matt that the way to approach people with the gospel isn't to tell them about what they can't do, but rather to introduce people to the one they need to know. "Matt, even if these people stopped drinking and partying, they are still bound for hell. Instead of telling them to stop drinking, tell them how to find Jesus."

Matt is not atypical. I can't tell you how many teenagers I have talked to who ran around pointing out rules, thinking they were being effective witnesses. If you want to be effective, concentrate on the main thing. People will not be saved when they stop drinking and give up all their bad habits. They will become new creatures only when they hear about Jesus and respond to his love.

Make It Attractive

I am convinced that the message of Jesus' love is very attractive. Everyone is looking for a loyal friend, and everyone has a need to be loved. And these are two things people will find in a relationship with the Lord.

God did not promise that all of life's problems would disappear as soon as someone prayed "the prayer." However, he did promise he would stick closer than a brother (Proverbs 18:24) and that he would walk through any circumstance with his children (Hebrews 13:5).

When you find the "felt need" in a person's life, you will have an opportunity to make the gospel relate to his or her life immediately. You can begin to tailor the conversation to how God can meet his or her specific needs.

If you are talking to someone who feels lonely, tell her about the relationship you have with Jesus that helps you through your loneliness. Has someone been abandoned? Tell him about Jesus. Are they in pain? Teach them how the Lord experienced pain and how he endured it for the opportunity to have a friendship with them. Then tell them how the Lord can help the healing process and ease the pain.

By making it relevant, you make it attractive. I am not saying you should embellish the truth, because the truth does not need embellishment. Any words you can use to describe the goodness of God and the great love he has for people won't come close to accurately describing God in all of his mercy. Tell the truth. The goodness of God and the love he has for the people you meet will captivate their hearts and open them up to the relationship that is available to them.

Pray for Them

If you are talking with someone about the Lord, don't end the conversation without making a verbal commitment to pray for them. If they are ready to make a decision for Christ, lead them in prayer right there. If they do not feel ready, but they are willing, pray with them anyway. If they are not willing to let you pray with them in that moment, tell them that you will be praying for them for the next few days.

Introduce New Christians to Mature Christians

If you have the privilege of leading someone into a relationship with Christ, his or her journey has just begun. Although your interaction with a new Christian may be ending, you should get him or her involved with some mature Christians who can begin discipling him or her.

If you share Christ with some friends and they receive him into their lives, you should begin to give them information about spiritual things. You need to teach them how to live for God and dwell in his presence. By building prayer into your friendship, including them in some of your church activities, or by buying them books that will help them, you will encourage them to get to know God and his plan for their lives.

If you are not regularly in touch with them, plug them into a church or introduce them to someone who can begin to invest in their lives. The very least you can do is point them towards a good church with a reputation for helping Christians mature spiritually. You could also help them by taking down their address and phone number and forwarding these to a church that is close to their home and will reach out to them. Be sure to communicate to the new Christians that their relationship with Christ has just begun.

Reality Check

- How can you remind yourself to be looking for opportunities to tell someone about Christ?

- Why do you think people need Jesus?

* How can you improve your question-asking skills?

* What do you think of the idea of focusing on just one person when addressing a group?

* What are some examples of minor things that may draw your attention from the "main thing" when talking with someone about Christ?

* What are some specific ways you can make the gospel attractive to people?

* What are some creative ways to get new Christians involved with mature Christians?

Father, I know *that you want me to be an effective witness and a pure testimony of your love and grace working in someone's life. Teach me how. God, birth in me a passion for souls and a heart that breaks for those who are walking separated from you. Make me willing to get out of my comfort zone and be inconvenienced so that I can share you with others. You have been so good to me and I don't know what I would do without you. May I never take you for granted. There is no name above your name. Amen.*

11

Learning to Disappear

"When a man is wrapped up in himself, he makes a pretty small package."

JOHN RUSKIN

In John 3:30, John the Baptist declared the mission statement for his life and ministry: "He must become greater; I must become less." Although John had multitudes coming to hear him and participate in his ministry, he did not let it go to his head. Everyone wanted his touch, but he knew he was nothing special. He was only the setup guy.

He had been given a job to do, and he would only be successful when he disappeared, and the Messiah shone bright.

To be really effective at making Christ known, you must take a page from John's book. You must learn to disappear. In this chapter you will learn about three things that kept John focused on his task. These same things will keep your motives pure as you seek to be used by God to impact your culture.

He Wasn't Swayed by Public Opinion

He didn't fit in. As a matter of fact, he stuck out like a sore thumb. When everyone else was wearing the latest fashions, he wore what was out of style. While everyone else was eating fancy foods, he refused to go there. Instead of following the crowd, he avoided them—until, of course, they began to pursue him.

John the Baptist will forever be remembered not for how he dressed, but for his calling, his message, and the God he served.

Rather than look to the latest catalogue to give him a feel for how he should dress, what he should eat, and how he should present himself, he found security in the Lord. "John's clothes were made of camel's hair, and he had a leather belt around his waist. His food was locusts and wild honey" (John 3:4). His outward appearance did not define him. John the Baptist will forever be remembered not for how he dressed, but for his calling, his message, and the God he served.

If you want to make a long-term impact for the Lord, find security in the Lord. If you are overly conscious about material things, you will not be fulfilling the great commission. If, however, you gain esteem from regular moments with the Lord and meditating on his thoughts about you, you will be able to take a radical stand for Christ.

Your clothes, cars, friends, or finances should not define you. You should be known for your heart, passion for, and obedience to the Lord. If you want to be remembered for your calling, your message, and the God you serve, like John is, you have to trust God with your image, and you can't be swayed by public opinion.

He Wasn't Trying to Climb the Ladder

Although John did not live a normal life, he did have a routine. One day while doing what was normal for him, some men approached him with a question. This visit presented an opportunity. If he answered correctly, he could have elevated his stock. If he was willing to go along with a false assumption, he could begin to make a name for himself. But John was not interested in gaining more notoriety. He was not looking for popularity or prestige. Rather than embracing the chance to climb, John answered as clearly as possible: "I am not the Christ" (see John 1:19–20).

Here was his chance. All he had to do to become the most popular man in all Israel was go along with the assumptions that had been made about him. However, he "confessed freely" he was not the one they were looking for. He was not looking to build his own kingdom, he wanted to advance the kingdom of the one who would come after him. He so eagerly awaited the Messiah that he almost bragged about the fact that he was not him. In a way John was saying, "It's not about me, I am nothing. However, the one that you are waiting for is coming, and he will change the world."

Many people in the church, both vocational ministers and zealous Christians, are trying to make a name for themselves. They long to have testimonies that will draw crowds. They manipulate conversations so that they can talk about themselves. If you are going to learn anything from John, remember that he didn't like talking about himself. He was uncomfortable with the acclaim he was receiving. His desire was to proclaim the message that had been laid on his heart. Only people who learn to disappear and point to Jesus will make a great impact for the kingdom.

John's Wish

John knew he was not the one with the answer, his job was to point to Jesus. He didn't want any of the credit or publicity. All he wanted was for people to know Jesus.

Only people who learn to disappear and point to Jesus will make a great impact for the kingdom.

[John said,] "I am the voice of one calling in the desert."
JOHN 1:23

[John] himself was not the light; he came only as a witness to the light.
JOHN 1:8

And this was [John's] message: "After me will come one more powerful than I, the thongs of whose sandals I am not worthy to untie."
MARK 1:7

[John said,] "Look, the Lamb of God who takes away the sin of the world!"
JOHN 1:29

John did not live a selfish existence. He knew who he was. He was just a voice. He did not shy away from this seemingly unimportant role, he embraced it. He knew who he was and he was not apologetic about his calling.

According to Scripture, you have a similar calling. You are an ambassador for the Lord; God is making his appeal to the world through you and others just like you (2 Corinthians 5:20). Do not turn away from this incredible invitation to be a part of building the kingdom of God. Recognize the calling of God that is on your life and don't apologize for who you are.

Only when you become less can he become more.

According to the world's way of measuring things, John was not successful. Instead of peers recognizing his accomplishments and applauding his resume, he was killed. When his life was over, the world thought they had rid themselves of an abnormal man with odd tastes and an absurd message. On the other hand Jesus recognized the world's loss and said, "Among those born of women there has not risen anyone greater than John the Baptist" (Matthew 11:11). Jesus said there was never anyone greater. Why? Why would John be so acclaimed by the one who knows everything? I believe the answer comes down to the fact that Jesus appreciated the desire of John's heart. John wanted to disappear because he knew Jesus should be the center of attention.

Make that the prayer of your heart. Ask the Lord to help you disappear as you live your life, share your faith, influence and serve others. Only when you become less can he become more.

Reality Check

- Your responsibility as a Christian is to point to Jesus, not to create attention for yourself. How can you instill this attitude in your heart?
- John didn't seem to care what people thought of how he looked. What are some possible reasons for this?
- How can you counteract a desire to be famous?
- What are some reasons for why you should not apologize for being Christ's ambassador?

You are a great God *and I am grateful to be one of your children. Lord, I pray that you would allow me to lose myself and my identity in you. I admit that you are able to protect my reputation. Lord, teach me to be content in my calling and not apologize for who I am or who you are in my life. And, most of all, may my life be so transparent that others see you in me. You must become more and I must become less. Teach me to live with this as the purpose of my heart. In the powerful name of Jesus, Amen.*

12

It's Your Destiny!

"Now with God's help, I shall become myself."
Søren Kierkegaard

He ran his whole life trying to accomplish something great, but in the end it was futile. He did not leave a legacy of greatness or impact. Rather, he left a sad tale of unachieved goals and untapped potential.

From a young age he had wanted to be a difference maker. He declared early in life that he would be a change agent everywhere he went. When he read about the great men of faith who had achieved so many things and had reputations of respect, he longed to be listed with them.

In the energy of his youthfulness, he was loud for the Lord, continually talking about the truth and forever sharing his beliefs about God. But as his age increased, his zeal decreased. When he was young, he could always be heard pointing others to Christ, but in his early twenties he developed a pattern of criticizing others and seeking fame for himself.

The change in his life was drastic—noticeable to all. It was apparent that he was not walking in love. He was not reaching out for the good of others. His shallow attempts to make a name for himself became visible to everyone, and he was thought despicable to the very people to whom he was trying to "minister."

Now he is forty-five and wondering where all of those years went. He asks himself, "Where is that young boy who wanted to impact others for Christ? Where did that selfless, loving part of me disappear to?"

As he wonders where his dreams of impacting the world for Christ went, he is confronted with a sad fact. He has wasted almost twenty years.

The years disappeared quietly but quickly. They slipped away under the veil of misplaced priorities and wrong motives. This lack of foresight led to the squandering of a destiny.

I Don't Want to Miss My Destiny!

As I write this chapter I am in Indiana speaking at a youth camp, and today I saw a shirt worn by a camper in the lunch line. It was not intended to be a spiritual shirt, but the truth of what was written on the back of it definitely applies to spiritual matters. The shirt said, "Your choices today will determine your success tomorrow. Choose wisely."

As you read this book, my assumption is that you want to know God and serve him. You want to know the voice of the shepherd, the embrace of the Lord, the things that concern his heart, and the thoughts that he thinks. There is also a part of you that wants to proclaim what you know about him. As much as you want to know him, you want to be used by him. You want to bring the "good news" to those you meet. You want your schools, your family, your friends, and your churches to experience what you encounter as you spend time with him.

Many young people are just like you. Thousands of people in this country want to know their Father and lead others to him. But many will never see their dreams realized.

Now is the time to decide. Your destiny is up to you.

Although they say the right things and their hearts cry out for them, many will miss out on their destiny and end up like the man I described in the beginning of this chapter. Why? Simply because of poor choices.

Your destiny awaits you. If you take time to get to know him, you will be effective at making him known. If you don't prioritize time for him, you will be another young person who lives year after year without stepping any closer to his or her original goal.

Now is the time to decide. Your destiny is up to you. Set a course for Jesus. Get to know him, and you will effectively make him known.

Forty-Five and Still Going

He has run his entire life wanting to be faithful. He has wanted to walk in intimacy with God and speak truth. He has left a legacy of integrity and impact. There are no sad tales of unachieved goals and untapped potential.

From a young age he decided to be a difference maker. He declared he would be a change agent everywhere he went. Rather than trying to gain the respect of people around him, he continually sought for his significance in the presence of God. His boldness came from knowing that God was pleased with him and watching out for him.

In his teens, twenties, and thirties, he was solid, ever ready to give an answer when someone asked him about his relationship with the Lord. Love was evident in his life and he continually crucified his pride and critical spirit. Because of his acceptance, patience, and love, people felt comfortable around him. He used every opportunity to speak of his faith and his friend, Jesus.

People had never seen anyone as sincere as him. It was noticeable to all around. The people he ministered to had seen many hypocrites that had turned them off, but his deep devotion mixed with his approachable nature broke down barriers.

He had a strong reputation of being a disciple of Jesus Christ and a minister as well. His faith and his life had impacted many people. His legacy was impossible to measure.

Now he is forty-five and wondering where all those years went. He does not ask himself, "Where is that young boy who wanted to impact others for Christ? Where did that selfless, loving part of me disappear to?" He sat at the Lord's feet and let God build him for the tasks that lay before him. He was faithful to spend time with God for the past thirty years, and it paid off.

As he takes inventory of the past and prays about the future, he is comforted with the thought that he is making a difference. Daily he is getting to know his Father, and daily he is making him known to the world. The past has been fulfilling, but he is positioned to make an even greater impact in the future.

He chose his destiny and is living his dream.

Will you?

Reality Check

- When it comes to your walk with God, what would you like your destiny to be?
- What steps can you take to make sure that you arrive at this destiny?
- What obstacles might prevent you from achieving your destiny, and how can you overcome these obstacles?
- What kinds of things would you like people to say about you after you've gone to be with your Father in heaven.

God, you created me *for a purpose. There is a very specific reason that you have placed me here on this earth. You want me to both know you and serve you. Lord, I pray that I would be consumed with the thought that I can know you more each day. Keep my motives right. May I never try and impress anyone with what I know or how diligently I serve, but may I continually give you all of the glory, honor, and praise. God, help me make my life count. May I live on purpose and with passion. I announce my love for you again. You are everything to me, and I give all that I am to you. In the mighty name of Jesus, Amen.*

For a free newsletter and a list of materials from Champion Ministries or for information on having Sean Dunn minister at your church, conference, retreat, camp, school, or other ministry group, please contact the ministry at:

Sean Dunn
c/o Champion Ministries
P.O. Box 1323
Castle Rock, CO 80104

Phone: 303-660-3582
Email: champion@championministries.org